*The Traveling Gourmets*

# Turtleback Farm Inn
# COOKBOOK

By
Denise and Michael Shumway
with
Susan and Bill Fletcher

Sweet Forever
Eastsound, WA   98245

Photo Credits:
Front cover food photo ©
by
Michael Skott

Inn photo
by
Jeffrey P. Buchner

Back cover photos
by
Friends

Copyright © 1990 by Sweet Forever.
Second Printing

All rights reserved.
No portion of this book may be reproduced without written
permission of the publisher.

**Library of Congress Cataloging-in-Publication Data**
Shumway, Denise, 1953-
    Turtleback Farm Inn Cookbook
    p.   cm. -- (The Traveling Gourmets)
Includes index.
ISBN 0-942133-60-9  :  $10.95
    1. Cookery--Washington (State)--Orcas Island. 2. Turtleback Farm Inn
(Orcas Island, Wash.)    I. Shumway, Michael, 1947-  .  II. Title.
III. Series: Shumway, Denise, 1953-       Traveling Gourmets.
TX715.S569      1990
641.5--dc20                                                    90-46734

Manufactured in the United States of America
Printed by BookCrafters, Chelsea, Michigan

Sweet Forever
P.O. Box 1000
Eastsound, WA  98245

# Dedication

For all of those who have slept in the shadow of
Turtleback Mountain.
                                        - Susan and Bill

————————————

To all of those who have shown us
that life is to be celebrated.
                                        - Denise and Michael

# Contents

*The traveler was active, he went strenuously in search of people, of adventure, of experience. The tourist is passive; he expects interesting things to happen to him. He goes "sight seeing."*
Daniel J. Boorstin, <u>The Image</u>

Food, people and philosophy go well together, as any good dinner party will confirm. One feeds the body; all three nourish the soul. This book is a letter about our travels and the food, people and philosophy we discovered along the way.

Michael and I call ourselves traveling gourmets. Between us, we have spent 20 years in the food industry. In that time we have lived and traveled over much of the United States. We do not refer to ourselves as gourmets, however, because of the length of time we have spent preparing and enjoying food. Nor does the adjective traveling mean to suggest that we are promoting tourism. If we promote anything, it is that life should be a pleasurable experience guided by education, open-mindedness, awareness and cultural exploration. We feel the word gourmet refers to more than an appreciation of food and wine. It can also refer to an appreciation of life.

Much of my approach to life comes from my uncle Ralph. Leaving home to travel at age sixteen, Ralph is still a wanderer 45 years later. His perspective is a little different from that of most people. He says that being a traveler is how life is meant to be lived; always observing, seeking out new places and ideas, balancing security and roots with adaptability and growth. He loves change. Each new location has a unique personality to him. He expects every place and everyone to be different, and he likes it that way. He is filled with stories of adventure and possesses the wisdom of an open mind.

Not everyone agrees with Ralph's lifestyle, but to us, he is something of a hero. Michael and I do our best to live as he taught us. We face the road with broad-mindedness. When beseiged by the unexpected, we remember that he told us we would rarely experience what we anticipated. But he also said that if we anticipate surprises, life will seldom disappoint us. We welcome the changes people and places bring us. The experiences we have far outlive our travels.

Food, culture and lifestyle are inter-related. All are best when varied, nourishing, explored and savored. This is the point of view we present to you.

In these pages, you will meet some of the people who have broadened us along the way with the food and ideas they have shared. We hope you find a good meal in these pages. And that it feeds you all over.

Denise & Michael

Orcas Island is a great place to take a fresh look at life. The people who live there are like most Northwesterners; friendly yet private, easy going yet hard working, independent and collectively protective of their environment. But there is a uniqueness about the islanders as well.

Certainly they are influenced by their environment. The landscape is beautiful enough to melt hearts and inspire artists. With its watery surroundings, gently rolling hills, pastoral valleys, huge stands of emerald trees and the clean air tinged with pine and sea breezes, the island feels primal, untouched by the ravages of modern civilization.

Articles written about the island often compare it and its people to some long lost time of simplicity. We found something beyond that. There is the feeling that the people who live there have taken the best of the past, its simple purity, and mixed it with the best of the new, an open-minded worldliness. The people of Orcas Island are not like the old man who, when asked on his hundredth birthday about the changes he had seen, responded, "I was agin every one of 'em." But they will question a suggested change, turn it over for observation and ask what the long term consequences will be.

These people are an eclectic bunch; former CEO's, professional artists and dancers, writers, wanderers, retirees from various professional persuasions, some rich, some poor. Even though there is only one small school on the island, with a kindergarten through high school population of less than 300, we found more informed and knowledgeable people there than in some towns with much larger populations. Talent abounds everywhere and the person waiting on your table or fixing your car may have expertise that might surprise you.

If we noticed one thing that seems to set them apart from "the people on the mainland," it is their easy going spirit and respect for one another. If you bring your city thinking with you and roar along the winding country road on someone's bumper, they will simply pull over and let you pass. Only a friendly wave will follow you. Most of these people seem to happily lack a "killer instinct." If you go into a restaurant expecting to buzz through as if you were at a hamburger chain, the staff may quietly remind you that life is a little easier here and that fresh meals made from scratch take longer than fast food duplication.

We suspect that if a survey was taken it would show many islanders view work as much as a means of self expression as anything else. And, like in most small towns, we experienced several examples of residents treating each other like family. There is the same rallying to support someone in need, the same open disagreement on issues big and small.

Part of what we appreciated about Orcas Island was its sense of community. We think when people talk about the good old days, they are not just missing a time with less pollution and stress. People long for this feeling of community; the caring about neighbors, acceptance of individuality and a feeling of safety. And we feel people miss living in communities where their voice can be heard and where they make a difference. It is our guess this is why there is an exodus going on in the United States right now, the so-called fifth migration, an exodus out of the suburbs and into small country communities. The challenge is to do what has thus far succeeded on Orcas Island and a handful of other communities around the country. That approach is a blending of the best of the old with the best of the new and an acceptance of individual lifestyles. Orcas Island hopefully is not a place that time forgot, but rather a glimpse of where we as a society might be headed.

Bill and Susan Fletcher, the owners of Turtleback Farm Inn,

are wonderful examples of the people who live on Orcas Island. They, like many people who find the island, were not looking for it. San Francisco Bay area residents, their original intent was to find a summer place. A tip from a friend lead them to the island. Once they arrived, plans changed.

A local real estate agent showed them a farmhouse on an 80 acre parcel of land. The original building was 85 years old and in great need of repair. In the recent past it had been used as a haybarn. A beautiful contemporary house on the back side of the parcel was the owner's home. Her husband, who had designed the house, had recently died. Not wanting to divide the land, she was selling it all or nothing.

Bill and Susan decided it was for them. The issue of how they would make the transition to their new home was a secondary concern. The decision was one from the heart, like that of many island residents. They would move to the island, then decide, once they got there, how to make a go of it.

The idea of transforming the old farmhouse into an inn presented itself weeks later. Against the backdrop of Turtleback mountain, the farm, with its gently, cascading emerald hills, six tranquil ponds, meadows, trees and flowers, created a place of breathtaking beauty and simplicity. The best of the old had survived on the farm. With the light mist in the mornings and the gentle afternoon sunshine, the land was a place where Bill and Susan found peace. They felt others might be in need of such a respite as well.

Orcas Islanders, well aware of the rarity of such a special place, guard the beauty of the island and do not take new buildings lightly. Bill and Susan, respecting the natural state of the land, decided to remodel the farmhouse and leave the area as much in its original state as possible. Many people would not have attempted such a project. It required dedication, vision and a willingness to work hard. Bill and Susan have all three. They met with the planning commissioners and builders. The results of their efforts to recreate the warmth and homeyness of the original building paid off. The redesign is spectacular.

On the inn's parlor table is a scrapbook which contains pictures of the remodeling process. Most guests are stunned when they see how the house looked before the transformation. All of the original farmhouse exists within the framework of the inn. Careful planning and design give the inn the peaceful, cozy feeling of a simpler time. Yet there is a clean elegance that speaks well of the present. The inn is a wonderful blend of the natural environment, the practical and the Fletchers' vision.

Bill did much of the redesigning himself. An artist at heart, he exemplifies the same sturdy self-reliance that you see in many islanders. Having worked as a master engraver for the government, Bill's eye for detail shows in careful accents throughout the house. He chose many of the colors and textures that create the inn's warmth. Braided rugs on the well-polished hardwood floors, gentle comfortable lighting and the soft crackle of a fire in the hearth combine to make one feel at home. Yet, the farm-like atmosphere is enhanced by the inn's touches of regional elegance; there are mirrors and crystal doorknobs from Seattle's grand old Savoy Hotel, and deep sinks and beveled bathroom glass from the regal Empress Hotel in Victoria.

Bill's experiences on his grandfather's farm in Virginia contribute to the ambiance at Turtleback. The eggs are gathered from Turtleback chickens. The comforters on the beds are lined with the wool of Turtleback sheep. Homemade jams, made from the farm's orchards, are often served with breakfast. Sitting in the dining room at the inn, we watched the sheep munching across the pasture, the chickens down in the yard scurrying from one curiosity to the next, and the ducks milling about the pond. Memories are rarely sweeter.

We thought that competing with the beauty visible from the dining room windows was no easy task, but Susan, the inn's gourmet cook, does it in stride. The rich aromas and heavenly flavors of Susan's wonderful breakfasts compliment the scenery nicely. Among her favorite recipes are crêpes smothered in island blackberries, cornmeal waffles, ham omelets or her famous homemade granola, which took the blue ribbon at the county fair. They all drew our attention away from the window to our other senses.

Susan reminded us of a younger Katherine Hepburn with her combination of world traveler sophistication and girl next door charm, wit and straightforwardness. The daughter of famed actor Buster Crabbe, she was raised in Hollywood. Her mother and father were a handsome, dashing couple, as attested by the pictures that hang in the inn and her home. The family was close knit. Her parents met when they were teenagers and remained virtually inseparable until his death several years ago. She and her mother often joined her father in various locations around the world. The experiences of travel at a young age show in the ease with which Susan responds to people and the unexpected situations that always arise in life.

In her culinary approach, there is the blending of the best of all possible worlds. Her menus often contain a wonderful mix of dishes. During one meal you might taste a unique combination of down home cooking and French cuisine. Yet the fare is always balanced. She insists on fresh, locally grown produce. She and Bill both appreciate the days when everyone grew their own food.

Susan is generous with her recipes. She had the granola recipe printed and sent out with Christmas cards. And when we asked how she put the zing in her homemade mustard or the pizazz in her Eggs Benedict, she did not hesitate to share. Having done a variety of entertaining in her life, Susan is comfortable preparing many types of dishes.

Although the inn is officially a bed and breakfast, Turtleback has been reserved for weekends by wedding parties. Susan also has done theme dinners for week-end groups. Her credo is that for a meal to be memorable, we must have a few surprises, but enough of the familiar to allow us to invoke trusting appetites. She says it takes flexibility in the kitchen, for one never knows when a little surprise will not turn out as expected. "Always have a back-up plan," she advises. "If you use fresh ingredients creatively, but stay within a menu framework, you can never go too far wrong. Serve the dishes unhesitatingly," she says, "your guests will feel relaxed because of your confidence."

Bill and Susan's confidence definitely influences the atmosphere at the inn. For all the inn's beauty, it was their sense of security which made it easy for us to relax. We felt safe there. Because they live in the house down the hill, we never felt that we had intruded upon their lives. They were always nearby when we needed them; then, they seemed to vanish into the woodwork, leaving us to our privacy and freedom. And although Bill was a country boy and Susan was a city girl, they have created a delightful composite style with the interaction of and respect for their differences.

Bill and Susan do best what all great hosts do - - they made us feel important. And we felt at home at the inn because they are so obviously at home with themselves.

# Scrapbook

*View of Turtleback Farm from the Fletcher's house*

*View of the San Juan Islands from Mt. Constitution*

*Our room for the night*

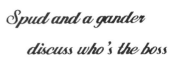

*Spud and a gander discuss who's the boss*

*Sheep shearing day at the farm*

*Susan's Oven baked Pancakes*

*One of the many*

*sailboats we saw*

*Inn parlor*

*View of Madrona Point from Crescent Beach*

Orcas was settled as a farming and fishing community. Turtle-back Farm is only one of many remnants of once active farm-lands. Among the islands chief crops was fruit. As we walked, biked and drove the island, we saw several still fruitful orchards. There are several ancient orchards, including one at Turtleback, still growing varieties of apples that are all but extinct in other areas of the country. In the fall, the county extension agent brings interested parties to the island to study the trees and sample the unusual fruits.

Another staple crop of the islands was strawberries. Many early settlers earned extra money as strawberry pickers and packers. A scant two blocks from the original ferry dock in Olga is the Artworks. The Artworks, a café and gallery housed in a re-furbished strawberry packing house, is a wonderful tribute to local talent and ingenuity. The gallery, a cooperative, displays and sells artwork by island craftpeople. Among the items are pottery, paintings, clothing, candles and ceramics. Far from being the typical gift shop items, these items are useful, elegant and just as the name implies, art, lovingly and skillfully created. We wonder how many other communities have such shops. We think it would be wonderful if other communities replaced the typical displays of ashtrays, drinking glasses and t-shirts with the efforts of its most talented citizens.

To give you an idea of the effort and quality put into these items, there are several hand-crafted pieces of wool clothing available. The wool is from sheep raised and sheared on the island, in several cases by the weavers who use it. These artists are so close to their product that they raise the sheep, then dye and spin the wool themselves.

Another type of art at the Artworks is the food in the café. The fare there is simple; fresh salads, sandwiches, quiches, home-made soups and pies. They are also known for their fresh baked cinnamon rolls. It is a wonderful place to go for a delicious lunch. Like Susan at Turtleback, the craftspeople who run the café make good use of local berries and fruits in their kitchen, and they put much of themselves into what they do.

Several of the local restaurants get their produce on the island from Rainwater Farms, an organic farm owned by Dennis George and Micky McGrath. Dennis is a farmer in the best sense of the word. He obviously loves his work, and raises an unbe-lievable amount of vegetables and flowers on a small amount of land. And he does it all organically. Micky is an artist. She paints and works in flowers. In her little shop in the village of Eastsound, she sells garden starts grown by Dennis and some of the most beautiful flower arrangements we have seen. They are only one of the many couples we met who own businesses on the island and work together.

There are also other farms on the island and strawberries are still a favorite crop. Strawberries and apples grow well on Orcas Island, the cool moist climate a natural for these fruits. But another berry has the honors when it comes to proficiency, the blackberry. Himalayan blackberries in the Northwest can al-most be compared to Kudzu in the South. These plants grow so fast that islanders who are "blessed" with the vines swear they can watch them grow. There are many jokes and stories, includ-ing Indian legends, about the almost indestructible plants. Mostly they describe the fate of those who paused beside the vines, only to find themselves engulfed by them in moments.

In the late summer and early fall, blackberry picking is at its peak. Because the vines grow wild along the roadway, opportu-nities are plentiful to help yourself to a handful. We observed bi-cyclists beside the road, picking a fresh fruit snack. As we stopped with them, it brought to mind several old sayings about taking the time to appreciate the simpler things in life.

If you want to pick a few berries, and you might once you see

Susan's recipes, there are a few things to remember.

Blackberries vines are feisty plants, not only because they take territory without hesitation, but because they do not willing give up their fruit for the favor of growing on your land. The berries are surrounded by prickly thorns which do not just prick, but grab. If at all possible, wear long sleeves and pants when picking berries. Gloves are also a good idea. And if you do get grabbed, do not pull away quickly, but gently remove the vine, one thorn at a time.

The berries are indeed black and soft when ripe. The deep crimson and blue ones, though, are too tart to use.

Susan loves to top things with the fresh berries. They add color to a plate, nutrition to the body, and delicious flavor to almost any dish including eggs. Any of the following recipes may be topped with berries, but they are especially good with the crêpes, the granola and the waffles, which are pictured on the cover.

Experts tell us that we're supposed to start each day with a full breakfast. At Turtleback, we make sure that our guests have that opportunity. Because breakfast is what we serve daily, the dishes we offer are tasty and unique without being so unusual that we miss the tastes of the majority of our guests.

Each day we offer at least two juices. Because they're so high in nutritional value, few items can serve as many needs as fruit and juice. We prefer fresh squeezed orange and pressed apple juices. In the fall, we offer juice from our orchard and when this is not available, we buy local fresh pressed juice.

We also prefer fresh fruits because they are higher in nutritional content and look and taste superior to canned or frozen fruit.

I am hesitant to give an exact number of servings with my recipes. Bill and I have raised eight children. Some of our children have large appetites while others have small ones, so I know only too well how serving sizes can vary. Please see the number of servings as a general guideline.

-Susan

> Being in the hospitality industry is like being a parent. You cannot be a part-time parent; nor can you be a part-time innkeeper. It is a very intense business. People have expectations. You must be genuinely interested in their comfort.
>
> -Susan

Zest is the outer rind or colored part of the citrus fruits. It contains oils which can enhance the flavor of many dishes. Zest can be removed with a vegetable peeler or julienned with a sharp knife. A zester is a tool that is made to remove long even strings of peel easily. Be sure to remove only the thinnest layer of rind. The white pith contains wonderful nutrients, but is bitter to the taste.

What we serve depends on what's in season. In the summer, I prefer melons and berries, including, but not limited to, strawberries, blueberries, raspberries and wild blackberries. I don't doctor the fruit with syrups or sugar. A good piece of ripe fresh fruit should be able to stand on its own. Finding it preferable to allow guests to sweeten the fruit to their tastes, I make sure there is honey or raw sugar on the table. In the fall, I bake apples and make applesauce, pearsauce and stewed ginger rhubarb. Many people are surprised to learn how tasty rhubarb is when served this way.

If I find I need to treat the fruit with a sauce to perk up the flavor, I use my favorite fresh fruit sauce. This is especially good on melon and can be used on fruit served for dessert.

# Fresh Fruit Sauce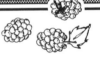

This recipe may be made omitting the rum.

*1/3 cup water*
*1 teaspoon lemon or lime zest*
*1/4 cup lemon or lime juice*
*1/2 cup honey or sweeten with honey to taste*
*1/2 cup light rum*

> Bring all ingredients except the rum to a boil, then simmer for 5 minutes. Cool.
> Add the rum. Refrigerate and use as needed.

# Baked Apples

This may be offered for dessert, served with vanilla ice cream and cinnamon to taste.

---

*6 baking apples, cored but not cut all the way through*
*3 teaspoons butter*
*1 1/2 cups brown sugar*
*3/4 cup water*
*3/4 cup orange juice*
*1/2 cup raisins*
*1/2 cup walnuts*
*lemon juice*
*cinnamon*
*nutmeg*
*light cream*

---

> Preheat oven to 350°.
> Take a circle of peel from the top of each apple, then poke the apple a couple of times with a fork so it does not explode during cooking. Fill the center of each apple with 1/2 teaspoon butter and pack very lightly with brown sugar.
> Give each apple a squeeze of lemon juice, then sprinkle with nutmeg and cinnamon.
> Put in a baking dish. Do not crowd.
> Put a handful of raisins and walnuts in the bottom of the baking dish with 1/2 cup brown sugar. Then add water and orange juice.
> Bake at 350° for 45 to 60 minutes or until soft when pierced with a fork. Baste regularly with the liquid.
> Serve warm with a pitcher of cream.

Serves 6.

The best apples grown in Western Washington for cooking are: Gravenstein, Summerred, Mutsu, Jonagold and Melrose. Some of the most popular varieties of apples sold in the United States are not grown here, but shipped from overseas.

The average amount of distance a food in the United States travels before it is eaten is 1300 miles.

**An apple a day keeps the doctor away.**
**American Proverb**

So cheek to cheek and
jaw to jaw,
 We sucked the cider
through a straw.
Pretty soon the straw
did slip;
 I sucked sweet cider
from her lip.
That's how I got me a
mother-in-law,
From sucking cider
through a straw.

# Applesauce Bread Pudding

This "dessert for breakfast" is great with bacon
or ham.

*8 slices of raisin bread*
*1/2 cup softened butter*
*1/2 cup raisins*
*2 teaspoons cinnamon*
*1 teaspoon nutmeg*
*1/2 cup brown or granulated sugar*
*1 1/2 teaspoons vanilla extract*
*3 cups milk*
*4 eggs*
*1 cup applesauce, preferably homemade*
*light or whipped cream*

>Preheat oven to 350°.
>Spread bread with butter and sauté on both
  sides until lightly toasted.
>Cut slices into quarters. Fit into a buttered
  9 inch X 13 inch baking dish.
>Spread applesauce on top. Mix the sugar and
  spices and sprinkle on top, then spread the
  raisins on top of the sugar-spice mixture.
>In a separate bowl blend milk, eggs and
  vanilla.
>Pour milk mixture over other ingredients in
  baking dish.
>Bake at 350° for 30-35 minutes. The pudding
  should be puffed and nicely browned.
>Serve warm with light or whipped cream.
Serves 6.

## Stewed Ginger Rhubarb

*8 stalks young rhubarb, sliced and trimmed*
*1 cup dark brown sugar*
*1 Tablespoon peeled, finely chopped ginger*
*1 1/2 teaspoons vanilla*

> The night before you want to serve this dish, fill a cooking pot with the sliced rhubarb. Rhubarb contains a lot of water and, if it is allowed to sit a few hours, will make its own cooking liquid.
> When ready to cook, add the brown sugar and ginger.
> Bring slowly to a boil over low heat. Simmer for 10 minutes and then allow to cool.
> Add the vanilla and serve warm or cool.

Serves 4.

Rhubarb leaves are inedible. Be sure to trim the stalks before cooking.

-Susan

## Green and Orange Compote

Occasionally, a guest will graciously share a personal recipe with me. This one was sent to me by Jeannie McMacken, who came to the inn on her honeymoon. It can be made up to 2 days ahead.

*2 cups apple juice*
*3 cinnamon sticks*
*8 cloves*
*1 cup fresh orange juice*
*4 granny smith apples, cut into 1/2 inch pieces*
*2 cups seedless green grapes, halved*
*8 navel oranges, sectioned*
*8 kiwis, peeled and cut into 2 inch pieces*

Citrus isn't the only good source of vitamin C. Other excellent sources are: peppers, broccoli, cabbage, brussels sprouts, greens, honeydew melons, cantaloupe, mangos, papaya and strawberries. Vitamin C is heat sensitive, so when cooking any of the vegetables listed above always expose them to heat as short a time as possible to reduce vitamin loss.

After our guests finish their fruit and cereal, we serve a main course. Each morning of a guest's stay, a different dish will be offered accompanied by either ham, bacon or sausage. As our guests check in, we always ask if they have any food allergies and whether or not they would like breakfast meat with their meal. Initially this was not a part of our check-in routine, but we shortly found that it is important to know of any dietary preferences or problems, just as you would want to know when you have guests in your home. We really did not need to know their car license number.

-Susan

Cup for cup, yogurt provides more calcium than milk.

> Bring apple juice to a boil with the cinnamon and cloves. Simmer for 15 minutes. Cool.
> Add orange juice and strain.
> Stir in all fruit and chill. Cover until ready to serve. Stores best in a glass bowl.

Serves 8-10.

# Turtleback Farm Granola

Turtleback Farm Inn Granola is always available. We serve it everyday along with the fruit and juice. Many types of granola that are mass produced are too full of sugars and tropical oils. That's unfortunate, because it can be a very healthful food if prepared right. The taste of this granola stands alone, but we serve it with raisins and yogurt on the side. This dresses it up as well as adds further nutritional value.

---

*4 cups rolled oats*
*3 cups whole wheat flour*
*1 cup white flour (unbleached)*
*1 cup shredded coconut*
*1 cup chopped nuts*
*1 cup wheat germ*
*1/2 cup cornmeal*
*1 cup oil*
*2 Tablespoons honey*
*1 cup warm water*
*1 Tablespoon salt (may be omitted)*

---

> Mix all ingredients well and spread into two 9 inch X 12 inch pans.
> Bake at 300°, stirring often to prevent scorching, approximately 60 - 90 minutes or until nicely browned.

# Cornmeal Waffles

*2 eggs, separated*
*2 cups buttermilk*
*1/2 cup unbleached flour*
*1/2 cup whole wheat flour*
*3/4 cup cornmeal*
*2 teaspoons baking powder*
*1 teaspoon baking soda*
*1/2 teaspoon salt*
*2 Tablespoons sugar*
*1/4 cup wheat germ*
*6 Tablespoons butter, melted*
*Pure maple syrup, warmed*

> In a blender at medium high speed, blend the egg yolks and buttermilk thoroughly.
> Add the melted butter and blend again.
> In a large bowl, mix the dry ingredients.
> Blend in the buttermilk mixture.
> Beat the egg whites until stiff but not dry. Fold them into the batter until just blended.
> Bake in a preheated waffle iron. Serve hot with warmed maple syrup and butter.

Serves 4.

Waffles stick to the grids of your waffle iron because of carbon buildup. The more sugar in your recipe, the more carbon buildup on your grids. To keep the iron seasoned but stick free, use a sparing amount of sugar in the batter.

The lightness of waffles depends on the airiness of the batter after the egg whites have been added. For best results take 1/4 of the beaten egg whites and stir into the batter then pile the rest of the whites on top of the batter, gently folding them in.

-Susan

# Crêpes

Crêpes are wonderful because they can be used in a variety of ways, both sweet and savory. You can fill them with chicken or tuna for lunch or dinner. (Recipes for these fillings are on page 73.)

At the inn, I serve at least two crêpes per person and offer seconds. Some of our children

> Ideally, crêpe batter should sit 2 to 3 hours before it is used. In all honesty, I have raced into the kitchen, blended up the batter and had crêpes cooked and on the table in a matter of minutes.
> 　　　　　　－Susan

> Earlier in my cooking career I always cooked with butter. Lately, however, I have been substituting margarine for butter because so many people are being cautious of their cholesterol intake. I find that in most recipes, margarine works fine, so make your own decisions concerning this substitution.
> 　　　　　　－Susan

can eat four or five without batting an eye. When serving them for breakfast, I top them with the berry sauce (recipe on this page) and a dollop of sour cream or yogurt.

*3 eggs*
*1 cup milk*
*1 cup unbleached white flour*
*2 Tablespoons melted butter*

> \>Mix all ingredients well in a blender and let batter sit. Batter should resemble heavy cream.
> \>Heat skillet over medium high heat. I use a 10 inch silverstone, sloping sided sauté pan. Add a little butter only before cooking the first crêpe. After the initial crêpe is cooked, you should not need to add more butter to the pan.
> \>While tilting the pan, add just enough batter to thinly coat the bottom of the pan.
> \>Cook until bubbles pop, about 1 minute. Turn over and brown second side.

Makes 8 crêpes.

# Fresh Berry Sauce

This sauce can be used for a variety of purposes, including desserts. I list it here for use with crêpes and oven pancakes.

*2 Tablespoons butter*
*3 Tablespoons sugar*
*1/2 cup orange juice*
*1 cup berries*

> \>Melt butter in a sauce pan.

>Add remaining ingredients and cook over medium heat until berries are soft.

If fresh or frozen berries are not available, an acceptable substitute can be made by substituting fruit jam for the berries and sugar, then heating it with melted butter and orange juice.

# Oven Pancakes

These are called German pancakes and have recently been added to the inn's repertoire. Because the inn's guests do not eat at one time, we cannot make a dish that serves everyone at the same time or that must be served immediately. After a bit of experimentation, I found it best to fill an individual au gratin oven proof dish with about 1/4 inch of batter and bake it in a preheated oven at 425° for about 10 minutes. It is done when you have a puffed up, bowl shaped pancake. Fill the center with fresh fruit and serve warm.

---

*3 eggs*
*1/2 cup white flour*
*3/4 cup milk*
*3 - 4 Tablespoons butter*
*pinch salt*

---

>Preheat oven to 425°.
>Mix eggs, flour, milk and salt well in a blender.
>Melt 1 Tablespoon of butter in each au gratin dish, then coat the dish with it. Pour 1/4 inch of batter into each warmed dish. Put into oven.
>Bake as above.
Serves 3 - 4.

The name strawberries originated in England, coming from the word straw, to cover the ground with scattered things. Strawberries grow wild in many parts of the United States.

German pancakes were made famous in the first half of this century by Victor Manca's Seattle restaurant, Manca's. His children called the dish "Dutch Babies." These pancakes can be filled with a variety of things and served for breakfast, brunch, lunch or dinner. It has its roots in Yorkshire pudding.

Some batters can be made ahead and stored in the refrigerator. For those whose mornings tend to be rushed, this is a great way to have a nutritious breakfast. Make a couple of batters on Sunday, one for muffins and one for oven baked pancakes, then your fresh breakfast can be cooking while you do other things. The exceptions to this suggestion are batters which contain baking powder.

-Susan

The strongest advice I can give new cooks is to read a recipe all the way through before beginning it. Many times I have made the mistake of racing ahead only to find myself midway through a recipe and knee deep in trouble.

-Susan

# Sourdough Pancakes or Waffles

The recipe for sourdough starter can be found on page 41. Starter must sit for several days, so be aware of this before starting this recipe.

This is a two part recipe and must be started at least 45 minutes before baking. Letting the batter sit overnight is preferable.

---

*1 cup whole wheat flour*
*1 cup white flour*
*1/2 sourdough starter at room temperature*
*2 cups warmed (100°) buttermilk*

---

>Mix all ingredients. If starting the night before, cover and put into the refrigerator until morning. Let the batter sit covered at room temperature until bubbly.

---

*2 eggs, slightly beaten*
*1/4 cup milk*
*1/2 cup oil*
*2 Tablespoons sugar*
*1/2 teaspoon salt*

---

>Mix together and add to the sourdough mixture. Let sit for a few minutes.
>Cook on a hot griddle for pancakes or a pre-heated waffle iron for waffles.
>Serve with butter and warm maple syrup or honey.
Serves 4.

# Whole Wheat Waffles

This recipe can be adapted for buckwheat or another type of corn waffle. The recipe changes are at the bottom.

---

*1 1/2 cups whole wheat flour*
*1 1/2 cups unbleached white flour*
*1 1/2 Tablespoons baking powder*
*3/4 teaspoon salt*
*1 1/2 teaspoons soda*
*2 Tablespoons sugar*
*6 eggs*
*3 cups buttermilk*
*1 cup melted butter or margarine*
*Warmed maple syrup*

---

>Mix together dry ingredients.
>In a blender, mix buttermilk, eggs and melted butter or margarine.
>Add dry ingredients to blender and mix until blended. If batter is too thick, thin with milk.
>Cook on a waffle iron according to manufacturers instructions. Serve with butter and warm maple syrup.
Serves 4.

### Buckwheat or Corn Waffles
*Use 3/4 cup white flour*
*3/4 whole wheat flour*
*3/4 cup buckwheat or cornmeal*
    *The rest of the ingredients remain the same.*

According to *Longevity* magazine, the three most powerful factors to long life that are within your control are:
> Where you live.
> What you eat.
> Whether you exercise.

**The two most basic and desirable qualities in food are flavor and texture.
...Pierre Franey**

Pancake batter which is too thick will cause the pancakes to be raw in the center. The secret to well done pancakes is thin batter. Also, some people prefer to add berries after the batter has been poured on the griddle. If your berries are frozen they may leave raw pockets in your pancakes. If the batter is too thin, you have probably left something out.

-Susan

The word farmer comes from the Latin word for ground, firma. Originally the term was applied to the owner of the land whether or not he worked it. After the 15th century, the term became associated with the one who tilled the soil.

# Berry Yogurt Pancakes

*1/2 cup white flour*
*1/2 cup whole wheat flour*
*1 teaspoon baking powder*
*1/2 teaspoon salt*
*4 Tablespoons sugar*
*1/2 teaspoon nutmeg*
*1 egg*
*1/2 cup plain yogurt*
*1/2 cup milk*
*2 Tablespoons oil*
*3/4 cup fresh berries, stemmed and sliced (Frozen, unsweetened berries can also be used.)*

>Beat together egg, yogurt, milk and oil.
>Mix together dry ingredients, then add
  to yogurt mixture. Gently fold in berries.
>Cook on a preheated griddle until bubbles
  form, turn and finish cooking.
>Serve with butter and maple syrup.
Serves 3.

# Banana Pancakes with
#              Honey-Nut Butter

*1 cup unbleached flour*
*2 teaspoons baking powder*
*1/2 teaspoon salt*
*1/8 teaspoon ground nutmeg*
*2 Tablespoons sugar*
*1 egg*
*1 cup milk*
*3 Tablespoons oil*
*1 cup mashed bananas (about 3)*
*2 teaspoons lemon juice*

>Sift together flour, baking powder, salt, nutmeg and sugar.

>Put the milk, egg and oil in a blender and blend at medium speed. Add in the bananas and the lemon juice and blend for a few seconds longer.

>Add liquid ingredients to flour mixture and stir until just combined. Batter may be a little lumpy.

>Place greased, seasoned griddle or large cast iron skillet over medium heat until a few drops of water dance on the surface.

>Pour a scant 1/4 cup batter for each cake. Cook on one side until bubbles begin to appear, edges look dry and the cake is fluffy. Then turn and cook the other side until golden brown.

>Serve at once with Honey-Nut butter.

Serves 3.

> The food that enters the mind must be watched as closely as the food that enters the body.
>
> ...Patrick Buchanan

## Honey-Nut Butter

*1/3 cup nuts (pecans are my favorite)*
*3/4 teaspoon orange zest*
*1/2 cup softened butter*
*1/2 cup honey*

>Spread nuts in a shallow pan and toast in a 350° oven for about 8 minutes. Cool. Chop nuts finely.

>In a food processor, process orange zest and butter until fluffy. Add honey and process until well combined.

>Add nuts and process until just blended.

>Serve at room temperature.

The honey-nut butter may be made ahead, covered and refrigerated.
-Susan

Cooking for people is theatre, as anyone who has worked in a restaurant will tell you. It is an involved performance.
-Susan

# Overnight French Toast

A favorite couple who stayed at Turtleback sent me this recipe. A very elegant and rich breakfast, I adapted it because we found it too sweet.

---

*8 pieces of homestyle bread, thinly sliced*
*1/4 cup melted butter*
*1/2 cup brown sugar*
*2 Tablespoons molasses*
*1/2 cup orange juice*
*5 eggs*
*1 1/2 cups milk*
*1 1/2 teaspoons vanilla*
*1 cup fresh berries*
*sour cream*
*1/2 cup walnuts*

---

> Mix butter, sugar, molasses and orange juice. Pour into a 10 inch X 13 inch pan. Tilt to cover bottom.
> Cover with 8 pieces of homestyle bread. You may want to double-deck the bread.
> Mix eggs, milk and vanilla in blender.
> Pour the mixture over the bread and refrigerate overnight.
> In the morning, preheat oven to 350°, then bake the mixture, uncovered, for 45 minutes or until nicely puffed and golden.
> Cut into servings and flip over into plate. Top with sour cream, fresh berries and a sprinkling of walnuts.

Serves 4.

For a different flavor add a teaspoon or two of Grand Marnier or rum to the French toast batter.

-Susan

When buying breads at the market, look for the words whole grain or whole wheat. Wheat flour is equal in nutrition to white flour.

# Fabulous-Fattening French

This recipe also works well with croissants.

*12 slices day old homestyle bread (can be raisin)*
*1 - 8 ounce package cream cheese, softened with a*
*    little milk added*
*3/4 cup half and half or milk*
*3 eggs*
*1/4 cup biscuit mix*
*1 teaspoon vanilla*
*apricot jam*
*oil for cooking*
*1 cup fresh berries*
*sour cream or yogurt*

> Spread 6 slices of bread with cream cheese and jam. Top with remaining bread slices to make a sandwich.
> In a blender, mix together remaining ingredients and pour into a pie plate.
> Soak sandwiches in batter on both sides until well saturated.
> In a wide frying pan, heat about 1/4 inch oil until medium hot. Fry sandwiches, a couple at a time, until browned and puffy on each side. Drain on a paper towel and keep warm until all are done.
> To serve, cut each sandwich in half, diagonally, and serve garnished with fresh berries and sour cream or yogurt.

Serves 6.

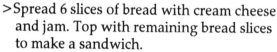

For variety, you may substitute thinly sliced ham and swiss cheese for the cream cheese and jam.

-Susan

We have always planned one morning a week that we sit in bed, sip coffee and catch up on personal business. Then we like to go out to a Champagne brunch, giving the morning as much of a celebrational atmosphere as possible.

There have been times when we could not afford the meal out, but did not want to spend our morning together in the kitchen cooking and cleaning up. During those times we had breakfast in bed with Champagne, homemade bread, cheese and fruit. We recommend this to anyone who wants to put a little romance into their relationship.

One of the most helpful hints I ever came across was given to me in a cake decorating class. It is a fool-proof preparation for greasing cake pans, bread pans, cookie sheets, muffin tins, etc. Mix together in a food processor; 1 cup flour, 1 cup crisco and 1 cup oil. Store this in a jar in the refrigerator and use to coat any surface before adding batter to the pan. It really works.

-Susan

# Sesame Corn Muffins

This recipe was given to me by my good friend Jan Helsell.

*3/4 cup unbleached flour*
*3/4 cup whole wheat flour*
*1/2 cup sugar*
*1 1/2 teaspoons salt*
*1 1/4 teaspoons baking soda*
*2 cups cornmeal*
*1 cup wheat germ*
*1/2 cup toasted sesame seeds*
*2 cups buttermilk*
*3/4 cup melted butter*
*2 eggs, slightly beaten*

>Preheat oven to 350°.
>In a large bowl, sift together flours, sugar, soda and salt. Stir in cornmeal, wheat germ and sesame seeds.
>In a blender, mix buttermilk, butter and eggs on medium speed until thoroughly blended.
>Pour milk mixture into dry ingredients. Blend just until moistened. Do not overmix.
> Pour into greased muffin tins,  2/3 full.
> Bake at 350° for 30 minutes.
Makes 12 muffins.

# Honey-Mustard
# Cheddar Muffins

One of the best things about breakfast muffins is that you can make enough for several days ahead and always have a quick breakfast.

---

1 cup unbleached white flour
1 cup whole wheat flour
1/2 teaspoon salt
freshly ground pepper to taste
1 Tablespoon baking powder
1 cup sharp cheddar cheese, grated
1 egg
2 Tablespoons Dijon mustard
3 Tablespoons honey
1 1/4 cups milk
1/4 cup melted butter

---

> Preheat oven to 400°.
>Combine dry ingredients in a mixing bowl.
>Whisk together the rest of the ingredients
   and gently, but thoroughly, fold it into
   the dry ingredients.
> Fill greased muffin tins.
>Bake at 400° for 20 minutes or until done.
Makes 12 muffins.

To make lighter muffins, place greased tins into the oven for a few minutes before adding the batter.

# Sour Cream Coffee Cake

---

1 cup soft butter
1 cup sugar
3 eggs, beaten
3 cups flour
1 teaspoon vanilla
1 cup sour cream
3 teaspoons baking powder
1 teaspoon soda
1 cup brown sugar
1 1/2 cups nuts, chopped
1 Tablespoon cinnamon
1 teaspoon nutmeg

A person who counts calories while enjoying a good meal, is like the person who thinks about business while making love. Calories should be counted before a meal is prepared, not while one is in the midst of it.
. . . Shumway's Law

**Biscuit Ideas**

Split them and fill with thin slivered ham, cornichon pickles, a bit of mustard and a few sprouts.

\* \* \*

Split them and fill with softened cream cheese and fresh jam or cream cheese with water cress or cucumber rounds.

\* \* \*

Serve them whole with an assortment of cheeses and fruits.

\* \* \*

Eat them plain with butter and honey.

\* \* \*

While they are still warm spread them with a tablespoon of the following mixture:
1 cup walnuts
1/2 cup marmelade
1/2 cup creamed butter
honey to moisten.

\* \* \*

Split and fill with egg salad.

>Preheat oven to 350°.
>In a bowl, mix together brown sugar, nuts, cinnamon and nutmeg. Set aside to use as topping.
>Cream butter and sugar. Add the eggs, then the flour and mix.
>Stir in vanilla, sour cream, baking powder and soda.
>Spread 1/2 topping into a greased tube pan. Pour 1/2 batter over topping. Spread remaining 1/2 topping over this and then add remaining batter.
>Bake 50 minutes. Let stand 10-15 minutes before serving.

# Biscuits

These biscuits are great for breakfast but also make a wonderful picnic bread. They work well for sandwiches if you make them large. To do this, make yourself a biscuit cutter from an empty tuna can. Wash the can thoroughly, being careful of rough edges. This cutter can be used for making English muffins or crumpets.

*3 cups unbleached white flour*
*1 cup whole wheat flour*
*1/4 cup unsalted butter*
*2 Tablespoons baking powder*
*3/4 teaspoon salt*
*2 cups heavy cream*

>Preheat oven to 375°.
>Process dry ingredients and butter in food processor until it resembles corn meal.
>Pour cream through feed tube and pulse until dough begins to form a ball, this should

take about 30 seconds.
> Knead on a lightly floured board about 10 times. Roll out and cut into rounds with a biscuit cutter. Place 1 inch apart on a lightly greased cookie sheet.
> Bake at 375° until puffed and lightly browned. Serve with butter and jam or honey.

# Sourdough Starter

Sourdough is a popular bread in the Northwest. Once you have starter available, it is also easy. Starter is not complicated to make, but it does require a few days to become active before you begin to bake with it. All you need is a few simple ingredients and a warm kitchen. My home is usually quite cool, so I don't make starter at home. I have gas ovens at the inn which are perfect for getting starter going.

Once you have starter, you only need to feed it regularly and you'll never need to make a new batch again. Below is the starter recipe. On page 43 is a recipe for bread made with sourdough. On page 32, is a recipe for sourdough pancakes or waffles.

---

1 cup skim milk
3 Tablespoons plain low-fat yogurt
1 cup unbleached flour

---

> Heat skim milk to approximately 95°, almost body temperature.
> Remove from heat and stir in yogurt.
> Pour into a 1 1/2 quart glass container. Cover it tightly.

Northwesterners love their coffee strong. All over Washington state you will find espresso stands which serve a variety of coffees and treats. The standard favorites are; espresso, an extra strong coffee prepared by a special machine through which steam under high pressure is forced; café au lait, equal amounts of strong hot french roast and warmed milk poured into a cup simultaneously; cappuccino , an Italian coffee made by adding a tiny amount of warmed milk and topping with milk foam; moccha, a strong coffee mixed with steamed milk and chocolate. If you do not have an espresso machine you can make café au lait, cappuccino by heating the milk, whipping it in a blender to simulate steamed milk, then adding it to strong brewed coffee. For a mocha, add chocolate to the milk while it is whipping.

**What hunger is in relation to food, zest is in relation to life.**
...Bertrand Russsell

Bread can be baked with their own brown crusts, or they can be glazed. The risen loaves can be brushed with milk or melted butter for a soft crust. For shiny crusts use an egg beaten with a tablespoon of water.

>Let stand in a warm place. (between 80° and 100°, no cooler or hotter.)

>After 24 hours, the mixture should resemble yogurt. If some clear liquid has come to the top, stir it back in; if the liquid is light pink, the milk has broken down. You should throw out the mixture and start again.

>Once your mixture has a yogurt consistency, add the cup of unbleached flour, stir until well blended and cover tightly. Return it to a warm place until it smells good and sour and the surface is all bubbly. This should take 2 to 5 days.

During this time if a clear liquid comes to the top, stir it back in. If the liquid is light pink, discard all but 1/4 cup of the mixture and blend in 1 cup warm skim milk and 1 cup flour. Let it sit again until warm and bubbly.

Your starter is now ready for use. Each time you use some of the mixture, you must replenish your supply. To replenish, you simply stir in equal amounts of warm, 80°-100° skim milk and unbleached white flour. If you do not use your starter regularly, throw half of it away and feed or sweeten it with equal amounts of warm milk and flour. If you do this regularly, every 10 days or so, you will always have active starter on hand.

# Classic Sourdough French Bread

Plan ahead if you want to make your own sourdough bread. Because you do not use yeast, but depend on the natural leavening action of the starter, the dough cannot be rushed.

---

*2 cups warm water (110°)*
*1 cup sourdough starter, let it come up to room*
  *temperature*
*4 cups unbleached white flour*
*2 teaspoons salt*
*2 teaspoons sugar*
*2 Tablespoons corn meal*
*3 cups unbleached white flour*

---

>Mix together 4 cups of the flour, water and the starter. Let it sit covered in a warm corner of your kitchen overnight, or at least 8 hours.
>When bubbly and spongy, stir in the salt, sugar and enough of the remaining flour to make a stiff dough. Knead either by hand or with a machine until smooth and elastic, about 10 minutes. Turn into a greased bowl and let rise until double in bulk, about 2 hours.
>Punch dough down and divide in half. Shape either into two round loaves or two long baguette shaped loaves. Put each one on a cookie sheet sprinkled with a little corn meal. Let rise again until almost doubled.
>Preheat oven to 400°. While oven is heating, slash the tops a couple of times with a sharp razor blade.
>Bake in the middle of the oven for 20 - 25 minutes.
Makes 2 loaves.

To simulate the old brick ovens, some people put a pan of water in the bottom of the oven while baking bread. I like to use a squirt bottle filled with water. Squirting the bread a few times during the baking process makes a wonderful loaf with a chewy crust.

-Susan

**We cannot become what we need to be by remaining what we are.**

**. . . Max De Pree**

Whole wheat bread does not have a hollow sound when tapped as an indication of being fully baked. White bread does.

-Susan

Milk is one of many liquids that can be used in bread making, but it plays an important role because of its nutritional value. Many old cookbooks directed the baker to scald fresh milk, because unscalded milk caused soft dough and interfered with the rising process. Pasteurization alters milk chemistry enough to prevent that effect so today few recipes call for scalded milk.

# Turtleback Farm
# Whole Wheat Bread

*6 cups warm water (80°-100°)*
*6 cups whole wheat flour*
*2 Tablespoons yeast*
*2/3 cup dry milk powder*
*2/3 cup potato flakes*
*1/2 cup rolled oats*
*1/2 cup wheat germ*
*1/2 cup corn meal*
*2 eggs*
*2/3 cup oil*
*2/3 cup honey*
*3 Tablespoons salt*
*8 cups whole wheat flour*

>Add yeast to water. Mix well until dissolved.
>Add 6 cups whole wheat flour. Mix well.
>Add remaining ingredients and enough of the remaining flour to make a stiff dough. Knead until smooth and non-sticky, about 7 to 10 minutes.
>Turn into a greased bowl and let rise until double in bulk. (I use a heavy duty mixer with a dough hook. For the first rising I leave the dough in the bowl to rise, covering it with a towel. When it has doubled, I turn on the motor and knead it a bit more with the dough hook.) If you do not use this method after the dough has risen, punch down and knead again.
>Divide into loaves. Put dough seam side down in greased bread pans and let rise again about 45 - 60 minutes.
>Preheat oven to 375°. Bake for 35-45 minutes, or until the bottom of the loaf is golden.
Makes 4 - 6 loaves.

# Turtleback Farm
## Whole Bran Muffins

I loved bran muffins even before the great bran debate. These are so tasty, they're worth eating for the flavor alone. And if they are good for you, so much the better. These are excellent with coffee or tea breaks. And for a light lunch, just add a slice of ham or some cream cheese.

---

1 cup 100% bran cereal
1 cup boiling water
3/4 cup honey <u>or</u> brown sugar
1/2 cup shortening
2 well beaten eggs
2 1/2 cups flour
2 1/2 teaspoons soda
1/2 teaspoon salt
2 cups buttermilk
1 cup All-Bran cereal
1 cup granola (Turtleback Farm Inn if you have it)
Optional: 1 cup raisins and/or 1 cup walnuts

---

>Preheat oven to 375°.
>Combine 100% Bran and water and allow to cool.
>Cream sugar or honey and shortening. Add eggs to the shortening mixture. Then add this mixture to the bran and water.
>Sift dry ingredients together. Add to the bran mixture in small batches, alternating with buttermilk.
>Add All-Bran and granola. At this point the raisins or walnuts can be added if you are using them.
>Fill greased muffin tins 2/3 full. Bake at 375° for 12-15 minutes.
Makes 18 muffins.

The batter for Whole Bran Muffins will store well for up to 8 weeks if placed in a sealed container in the refrigerator.

-Susan

Good communication is as stimulating as black coffee, and just as hard to sleep after.
... Anne Morrow Lindbergh

I prefer raw milk cheddar cheese above all the other cheeses I have tried for cooking. It is not overly colored, has the best flavor and melts smoothly without being too chewy.

-Susan

**Egg Tips**
A fresh egg will hold together better when poaching. Older ones tend to separate and are not as flavorful. Never leave eggs, raw or cooked, out of the refrigerator for more than two hours. Refrigerate eggs in the carton, they are probably more sanitary than your refrigerator shelf. Also eggs should not be stored uncovered as they absorb odors and lose moisture.

# Mexican Eggs

I usually serve these with corn muffins and ham. When allowed to cool and cut into squares, they're also great for appetizers.

*1 -4 ounce can whole Ortega chilies*
*1 pound grated raw milk cheddar*
*1 1/2 cups milk*
*5 large eggs*
*1 Tablespoon flour*

> Preheat oven to 375°.
> Butter the bottom of a 10 inch glass pie pan, or a 9 inch x 13 inch rectangular one if you want to cut into squares.
> Arrange chilies on the bottom of the pan and top with grated cheese.
> Blend remaining ingredients in a blender and pour over cheese and chilies.
> Bake at 375° for 45 minutes or until puffed and golden. Serve with a dollop of sour cream, a sprig of fresh cilantro and a slice of tomato on top. Offer fresh salsa on the side.

Serves 6.

# Fresh Salsa

Salsa adds zip to any egg dish, be it simple scrambled eggs or a breakfast quiche. This is my favorite salsa recipe.

*3 or 4 ripe tomatoes, chopped*
*1/3 white onion, finely chopped*
*1 clove garlic, minced*

*3 or 4 fresh sprigs of cilantro, remove stems and chop*
*1 serrano chili, finely chopped*
*salt, pepper and fresh lime juice - to taste*

> Blend all the ingredients together and let flavors develop for 1/2 hour before serving.

# Eggs Benedict

*4 English Muffins*
*8 small slices of ham*
*8 eggs*
*cayenne pepper*
*Pam*
*1 teaspoon vinegar*

> Split English muffins and toast. Warm ham.
> Spray a flat bottomed pan with Pam. Fill half full with water and bring to a simmer on stove top. Add a teaspoon of vinegar to the water, this will help congeal the eggs. Break the eggs into a cup, not into the pan. Swirl the water around, then gently place the eggs to be poached, into the pan. Judge doneness by tapping the eggs lightly with the edge of a spoon.
> Layer a slice of ham, a poached egg and hollandaise sauce on top of each muffin half. Sprinkle with cayenne before serving.

Serves 4.

## Hollandaise Sauce

*2 Tablespoons of butter, cut into thirds*
*3 egg yolks*
*1 Tablespoon fresh squeezed lemon juice*

The grade on egg cartons indicates freshness not size. Grade AA eggs are fresh fancy; Grade A eggs are good in appearance and flavor and can be used for most dishes; Grade B eggs should be used only for general cooking and baking.

**Love and eggs are best when they are fresh.**
**...Russian Proverb**

The shell of the egg is a result of pigment, the yolk color that of feed. A fresh farm egg, produced by chickens who are well fed, will have a deep orange-yellow colored yolk.

> In the top of a double boiler, melt the first 1/3 of the butter cube. Whisk. Add second 1/3 and melt, whisk. Add last 1/3 to melt and whisk. Whisk in yolks and lemon juice.

---

## Ian's Cheese Eggs

Ian is the youngest of our children. He is also a boy scout and very self-sufficient. When he has friends over for the weekend he likes to cook breakfast himself. Here is his recipe for cheese eggs. This dish is a favorite among teenagers, but not recommended for those on low cholesterol diets.

---

*4 eggs*
*4 Tablespoons milk*
*2 Tablespoons butter*
*handful grated cheddar chesse*

---

> Beat eggs with milk.
> Melt butter in non-stick pan.
> Add eggs, scrambling over low heat, stirring constantly.
> When partially cooked, add the cheese and finish cooking.

Serves 2.

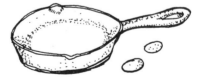

---

Low heat is essential in cooking any mixture enriched with egg yolks. If your sauce separates, it is because it is too hot. You can rescue it by whisking in 1-2 table-spoons of cream, or another egg yolk.

-Susan

Flowers are a wonderful garnish for egg dishes. Choose edible, pesti-cide-free unbruised va-rieties. Some favorites are borage, pansies, primroses (except Chinese primroses), lavender, nasturtiums, roses (petals only) and violets.

# Fresh Mushroom Omelet

Omelets are fun to make. They make a wonderful breakfast or a tasty dinner. With a basic omelet recipe you can experiment, adding new fillings as your imagination allows.

*10 eggs*
*3 Tablespoons water*
*1 pound mushrooms, sliced*
*1 Tablespoon snipped chives or 2 scallions, chopped*
*2 Tablespoons butter*
*1 Tablespoon fresh rosemary or 1 teaspoon dried*
*1/2 pound grated swiss or cheddar cheese*

> Beat eggs in a blender with water. Do not overblend.
> Melt butter in a large frying pan and sauté mushrooms with chives and rosemary until the mushrooms begin to give off their liquor. Keep warm as you prepare omelet.
> Melt 1/2 teaspoon butter in an 8 inch frying pan (non-stick is best). Heat butter until bubbly, then add enough eggs to cover bottom of pan about 1/4 inch thick.
> Push eggs with spatula to center as you tilt pan, enabling uncooked eggs to flow over the set eggs. When almost done put a line of mushroom mixture down the center of omelet then add a handful of grated cheese.
> Fold the right then the left side over filling. Serve hot.

Makes 4 omelets.

**Suggested Omelets:**
chicken & tomato
sweet peppers & onion
sautéed potatoes & ham
asparagus & shallots
spinach & bacon
crab & asparagus
fruits in fruit sauce
cream cheese & jam

### He that travels much, knows much.
... Thomas Fuller

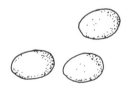

**The tongue of a wise man lieth behind his heart.**
Ali Ibn-Abi-Talib

# Quiche

Many cooks today buy frozen prepared shells for quiches and pies. Although the shells will work, I find them inferior to a homemade crust because they often break and can become soggy while cooking. Some cooks feel pie crust is too difficult and are hesitant to try. But, if you know a few simple tricks, you can make a flaky crust every time. And if you want, you can make several and freeze them for convenience.

### Crust Recipe

*3 cups flour*
*1 cup crisco*
*pinch salt*
*4 Tablespoons cold water*

> Preheat oven to 350°.
> Cut the crisco into the flour using a food processor.
> Add water and salt.
> Roll the dough out carefully on a floured surface. The less you handle the dough the better. Overhandled dough has been stretched and will pull back when baked.
> Place dough into pie pan and flute the edges. Prick all over with a fork, especially the sides of the shell. This releases steam so the crust will not crack.
> To prevent the crust from becoming soggy, bake blind. First place a piece of wax paper along the bottom of the crust. Then cover with a handful of dried beans. This weights the crust down. Then bake for 15 minutes, unfilled. Allow to cool.

## Basic quiche recipe

*1 1/2 cups half & half*
*4 eggs, beat slightly*
*1 Tablespoon dijon mustard, this is a maximum, use*
    *less if preferred*
*pinch nutmeg*
*1 cup grated raw milk cheddar*
*1 cup filling of your choice*

> Preheat oven to 415°.
> Beat half and half, eggs, mustard and nut-
  meg together.
> Line the bottom of the crust with your filling
  choice. My family prefers Quiche Lorraine,
  which is made with chopped ham. Other
  possibilities are listed in the margin. Cover
  your filling with cheese. Then pour liquid
  mixture over top.
> Bake for 10 minutes, then reduce oven tem-
  perature to 375°. Cook for 40 minutes. Check
  for overbrowning. If the quiche browns too
  much, cover the top with aluminum foil.
> Let cool for 10 minutes before cutting. This
  allows the quiche to set so it cuts clean.

**Quiche suggestions:**
sautéed mushrooms
smoked salmon
flaked crabmeat
red & green peppers
broccoli
shrimp
spinach & bacon
asparagus & chicken

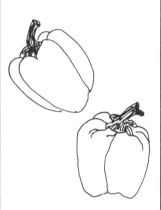

# Soufflé Roll

The filling for the soufflé roll works great in
an omelet.

*4 Tablespoons butter*
*1/2 cup flour*
*1 teaspoon salt*
*pinch pepper*
*2 cups milk*

This can be prepared
ahead and stored
overnight in the
refrigerator. Warm
thoroughly in the oven
or microwave before
serving.
                    -Susan

5 egg yolks
5 egg whites

**Filling:**

1 bunch spinach, cleaned, stemmed, chopped, or 10
    ounce frozen chopped spinach
1/2 pound mushrooms
2 Tablespoons butter
8 ounces cream cheese
pinch salt
pinch pepper

> Preheat oven to 400°. Have all ingredients ready as filling will be made while soufflé is baking.
> Melt 4 Tablespoons of butter in a saucepan. Blend in flour, salt and pepper.
> Whisk in milk, bringing the mixture to a boil. Stir constantly until thickened.
> Cool. Add the egg yolks, one by one, and beat.
> Beat the egg whites until stiff. Fold them into the cooled sauce.
> Line a jelly roll pan with waxed paper, then butter and flour it. Pour in the soufflé mixture, spreading lightly to form an even layer.
> Bake for 30 minutes or until nicely browned.
> Turn immediately onto a towel.
> While soufflé is baking, sauté spinach and mushrooms in 2 Tablespoons of butter until tender.
> Add the cream cheese and mix well. Season to taste.
> Spread the warm filling evenly over the warm soufflé and roll up jelly roll style with the help of a towel.
> Serve immediately.

Life is a great big canvas, and you should throw all the paint on it you can.
. . . Danny Kaye

# Washington's Best Loved Fruits

**Apples** - All strains of apples listed store well except Gravensteins, which should be eaten within two weeks of picking. Apples store best in a cool, dry, dark place such as a cellar. Below are some Washington state apples, their seasons and their uses.

| | | |
|---|---|---|
| Gravenstein - large, light green and red strains | | |
| sweet and juicy | early Sept. | cooking & eating |
| Summerred - dark red with speckles | | |
| tart, firm, fine texture | Aug. thru Sept. | cooking |
| Mutsu  - large yellow-green | | excellent |
| juicy, crisp, spicy tart | Oct. - Nov. | cooking |
| Spartan - red with pure white flesh | | |
| mild, juicy and crisp | Oct. | eating |
| Jonagold - large yellow with red stripes | | |
| crisp and juicy | Oct. | eating |
| Liberty - red stripes on yellow background | | |
| crisp, juicy and sweet | late Sept. | eating |
| Melrose - large, quiet red | | excellent |
| sugary sweet, slightly tart | Oct. - Nov. | eating & cooking |

**Pears**   Pears are ripe if the stem end gives a little when pressed. Select firm, slightly underripe pears and let them ripen in a bowl or paper bag. Slightly underripe pears are best for cooking. Pears become overripe quickly, so use soon after ripening.

| | | |
|---|---|---|
| Bosc - long necked, russet hue over golden skin | | |
| tart flavor, buttery texture | Oct. - May | cooking |
| Bartlett - large and bell shaped | | |
| sweet, musky flavor | Aug. - Nov. | eating |
| Anjou - russet colored, egg shaped | | |
| sweet, wine-like flavor | Oct. - May | cooking & eating |
| Comice - round and green | | |
| sweet and juicy | Oct. - May | eating |

**Berries** - Berries are very versatile and can be used for garnish, sorbets, ice creams, parfaits, tarts, cobblers, pies, muffins, jams, sauces, wines, vinegars, chutneys, or served fresh. Unless frozen, berries should be refrigerated and eaten within a week. The favorite berries grown in Washington and their seasons are blackberries (July - Sept.), strawberries (April - July) and blueberries (June - Aug.).

# Cheeses

Since Washington is first among all 50 states in milk production, a thriving cheese industry exists there. And the cuisine-conscious producers do not stop with cheese made from cow's milk, but use goat's and sheep's milk as well.

Commercial cheesemaking in the Pacific Northwest began in Tillamook, Oregon in 1899 and focused on the traditional cheeses such as cheddar, colby and Swiss. Today there is a wide selection of cheeses including Quark, a soft yogurt/cream cheese mixture, and a variety of cheddar cheeses with flavorings of linguisa or chorizo added.

Some of the limited-production Washington cheeses are sold in supermarkets, sometimes under regional rather than brand names. If your supermarket does carry a particular type, look in specialty cheese shops, fancy food stores and health-food stores throughout the area.

Below are some cheeses and their uses.

**Blue** - French origin; tangy sharp; appetizer, salad and dessert.

**Cheddar** - English origin; mild to very sharp; snack, cooking and dessert.

**Edam, Gouda** - Dutch origin; mild; appetizer, snack and dessert.

**Provolone** - Italian origin; can be smoked; mild to sharp; cooking and snack.

**Brie** - French origin; mild to pungent; appetizer, dessert.

**Cream** - U.S. origin; very mild, chill slightly; salads, snacks and dessert.

**Ricotta** - Italian origin; mild, curd or dry; cooking and dessert.

**Mozzarella** - Italian origin; mild; cooking, snacks.

**Roquefort** - French origin; sharp, salty; appetizer, salad and dessert.

**Swiss** - mild, nutty, sweet flavor; appetizer, sandwich, cooking and dessert.

**Monterey** - California origin; mild; appetizer, cooking, sandwich.

# The Pig War

Orcas Island is one island in a chain of 473 (at high tide) known as the San Juans. These islands are located in the Strait of Juan de Fuca and are a part of Washington State.

Originally, the islands were claimed by both Great Britain and the United States. Both sides agreed that the 49th parallel up to Point Roberts at the sea was the boundary between United States and British territories. At Point Roberts, they disagreed which of two channels the line should follow. The British proposed that the line follow Rosario Channel, which would have made the San Juans a part of British Columbia. The Americans wanted the line to run through De Haro Straits, making the islands a United States territory.

Both countries kept troops posted in the area, creating a conflict of authority. It was commonplace for those accused of crimes by one side to claim protection from the other. For this reason, the islands soon became a gathering place for outlaws.

Many settlers in the San Juans were former employees of the Canadian owned Hudson Bay Company. The company conducted fur trade in the area, employing men from American territories and Canada. Company policy encouraged employees to take Indian wives, both to obtain control of trade and to insure against uprisings. These Native American women were purchased for prices ranging from $20.00 to $50.00 according to looks and social standing in the tribe. Men who married these women were called "squaw men."

In 1859, an American settler named Lyman Cutler became frustrated by a Hudson Bay Company pig that had broken down his fences and rooted his garden. He killed the pig with his rifle, then felt remorseful and went to the company to make restitution. He asked the clerk what the pig was worth and was told it was a prize breeder worth $100.00. With the best wives going for $50.00 and whole farms for $200.00, Cutler thought the price was too high and refused to pay.

Both sides claimed injury in the incident. The United States sent in troops to settle the matter and the British countered with war ships. Hotheads on both sides demanded war, but fortunately cooler heads prevailed and the issue was settled through mediation. Because the only casualty of the confrontation was the pig, the incident came to be known as "The Pig War."

Several years passed before the boundary matter was settled, however. In 1872, the German Kaiser was called upon to decide the boundaries and settled in favor of the United States. A reasonable time was given to the claimants of land in the area to settle their affairs.

As a side note, the Hudson Bay Company's interest in the San Juan Islands was primarily in mink, which were trapped to extinction in the area.

Turtleback Farm is a working farm. The Fletchers do not plant a crop each year to take to market, but they do tend their orchards, raise chickens and sheep and harvest hay. They also cultivate gardens. Many wildflowers graced the farm before the Fletchers came, but the flower gardens they have established since their arrival are breath-taking.

Being raised in the city, I had little exposure to flower gardens as a child. I think that Michael was lucky; he grew up on a farm. I have always thought that growing up in the country, with clean air and water, wide open spaces and a horse or two, was idyllic. Michael agrees it was wonderful, but points out that a farm is a lot of work.

I found that out when I planted my first garden at the age of twenty-two. It consisted of a few fruits and vegetables because I considered myself a practical person; flowers to me were not practical. Fully into the experience I canned fruit, made pickles and jams and froze vegetables. The garden gave me a huge return for my work, but it was years later before I understood the practical side of beauty.

Recent studies by Japanese researchers have shown that flower scents delivered throughout large building via air-conditioning systems have the power to soothe the weary, lessen mental fatigue and induce calmness. Perhaps this is our unconscious motivation for giving one another flowers and perfumes. Far back into recorded history people have given flowers as symbols of victory, prosperity and admiration. Although we are not sure what our distant ancestors knew about plants that brought about this gift of flowers, we are coming to understand more fully the gifts that plants give us.

Plants have always been known for their food value. Fruits,

nuts, leaves, roots and flowers are all common to the human diet. For centuries, among various cultures including those of western civilization, flowers and herbs were a staple. Even today, cooks include flowers in their menus without realizing it. Broccoli, cauliflower and artichokes are flower buds, as well as common foods. Marigolds, borage, gladiolus, lilacs and nasturtiums are not often used today, but for centuries these flowers were as common to the diet as broccoli is now.

Chrysanthemums were a part of Confucius' diet. Greek historians tell us that the Persians ate nasturtiums. The Romans and the Greeks celebrated enormous banquets that included rose petals and violets. When cooking became fashionable in seventeenth century Europe, obtaining, preparing and preserving food was not a simple matter. Fresh fruits, meats and vegetables were not readily available. So, flowers, spices and herbs were heavily relied upon.

These ingredients were known to have medicinal properties, as well as food value. Earlier cultures knew that food is more than just something to satisfy the appetite. The word restaurant comes from the same Old French word that gives us the words restore and restoration because early inns served hearty broths that were known for their healing properties. Even today, some remote cultures have practicing herbalists, and scientists are discovering anew the healing properties of food.

Michael and I had our first experience with flower cuisine in a restaurant. When our plates were brought to the table, they were beautifully garnished with nasturtiums. After we expressed hesitancy about the wisdom of this, the server assured us that they were safe to eat. She also told us that the flowers are high in vitamin C and contain a herbal type penicillin that helps ward off infection.

Since that meal we have seen flowers in many kitchens and I have planted a flower garden. Flowers contribute to the beauty of a salad, add an unusual taste to soups, float gracefully in a glass of wine, and garnish a cake beautifully.

In recommending flowers for the kitchen, we suggest that you grow your own. Many flowers bought in stores today contain chemicals which are not safe to eat. If you do buy flowers from a local florist or nursery, be certain they are organically grown. Before using, always wash the flowers gently to rinse off any dirt or residues.

When we first tried flower cuisine, we were a little nervous because we know powerful medicines come from flowers. Poppies are the source of a number of pain killers and foxglove gives us heart medication. Our ancestors were not ignorant because they used botanical medicines, we still do. Unfortunately, many people are not as familiar with nature as their grandparents.

But we learned there are many ways of finding out which plants are safe to eat and which ones are too powerful for our systems. We found books at the library which helped us identify the flowers which are safe in a given area. *Field Guide to Edible Wild Plants* by Angier is an authoritative guide to plants and their habitats in the United States and Canada. *The Edible Wild* by Berglund and Bolsby and *Stalking the Wild Asparagus* by Gibbons may also be helpful. If you are interested in finding out about plants in your area, the county extension agent may shed some light on the subject. We found our local nursery quite knowledgeable. Botany departments of local schools may also provide information. On Orcas Island, two local residents give annual walks through the woods to identify which plants are edible. Perhaps a botanist in your area gives such a tour. Animals also provide us clues to what is edible, but because their systems are different, they are not a foolproof barometer.

On Orcas Island, because there are no natural predators, the local deer feel safe eating out of your hand. They also help themselves to residents' flowers. Gardeners grumble good naturedly about it and put high fences around their prize vegetable and flower gardens. The deer, however, have the good sense to know which flowers are unhealthy. On Orcas, these are the ones growing undisturbed along the roadway.

In the next two recipes you can substitute half & half or yogurt for the sour cream to reduce calories and cholesterol.
-Susan

**He that is of a merry heart has a continual feast.**
...Proverbs 15:15

# Soups

From time to time, I have fixed picnic baskets for honeymoon couples. These soups are great thermos fillers. They are especially good with sourdough bread. If you bring along fruit and cookies, you have a complete meal.

## Summer Beet Soup

*3 medium to large beets, unpeeled and scrubbed*
*4 cups buttermilk*
*2 cups sour cream*
*1/2 cup lemon juice*
*1/2 cup finely minced scallions, tops and all*
*2 large cloves garlic, minced*
*salt*
*pepper*
*1 lime, thinly sliced for garnishment*

> Cook beets in boiling water until very tender when pierced with a fork, about 45 minutes. Drain and allow to cool until they can be handled.
> Slip off the skin and cube the beets finely. Set aside 3/4 cup for garnish.
> Using a blender or a food processor, purée the beets in the buttermilk until smooth.
> In a large bowl, mix the beet purée with the sour cream, lemon juice, scallions and minced garlic. Season to taste. Whisk until completely blended.
> Add the reserved beets and chill overnight.
> Before serving taste for seasoning, adding

more lemon juice if needed. Garnish with a lime slice.

---

# Cucumber Soup

---

*2 cucumbers*
*1/4 cup chopped parsley*
*1 leek, white part only*
*1 pint sour cream*
*1 teaspoon salt*
*2 Tablespoons lemon juice*
*4 cups buttermilk*
*2 Tablespoons fresh dill, for garnishment*

---

>Peel, seed and chop cucumbers except for six thin slices to be used for garnish. Put half the cucumber in a blender with half of the leeks and parsley and 2 cups buttermilk. Blend until smooth. Remove from the blender.
>Repeat with the remaining cucumber, parsley, leeks, buttermilk and salt.
>Blend the two mixtures together. Whisk in sour cream and lemon juice.
>Chill until serving time. Add the dill and cucumber as you serve.

---

# Gazpacho

---

*1 clove garlic*
*2 teaspoons salt*
*1/2 cup chopped mushrooms*
*3 Tablespoons olive oil*
*1 cup scallions, finely chopped, tops and all*

**Suggested Garnishes:**
almond slivers
diced apples with skins
avocado slices
thinly sliced carrots
cauliflower buds
chopped celery
grated cheese
sour cream
chopped fresh herbs
sliced olives
orange peel
thinly sliced radishes
small cooked shrimp,
   deveined and shelled
diced tomato
chopped scallions

On a picnic, or when brown bagging to work, plan on eating light. A touch of something unique will break up the lunchtime doldrums and leave you feeling satisfied better than a large amount of food. Then you are not faced with leftovers or that sleepy, too full feeling at mid-day.

**How to dry flowers**

Pick blossoms just before they open  and place in cool water overnight.

Pour an even one inch layer of fine dry sand into a large flat box. Gently dry the flowers with a towel and remove any leaves. Place flowers on the sand without allowing plants to touch each other. Cover completely with sand.

Cover and set box in a warm dry place and allow flowers to dry completely. To store flowers, hang them upside down or stand them upright in a vase.

*2 cups tomatoes, finely chopped*
*1 cup red or green peppers, finely chopped*
*1 cup cucumber, peeled and finely chopped*
*2 teaspoons chives*
*1 Tablespoon chopped parsley*
*1 teaspoon finely ground pepper*
*1/4-1/2 teaspoon tabasco*
*1 teaspoon Worcestershire sauce*
*1/2 cup tarragon wine vinegar*
*3 cups tomato juice*
*lemon juice to taste*

>Crush garlic in the salt.
>Sauté mushrooms in olive oil until just lightly browned.
>Combine all the ingredients together. If you use a food processor, be certain to chop the ingredients, not purée them. Do not use a blender. Cover and chill over-night. Use a glass or stainless steel bowl for storage, not an aluminum one.
>When ready to serve, correct the seasoning, adding lemon juice and seasoning to taste.

# Mushroom Soup

This soup resembles a cream soup as it is quite thick. The advantage is that it is the real thing - mushroom soup without the cream or flour thickeners often found in cream soups.

*1 1/2 pounds mushrooms, chopped*
*2 Tablespoons butter*
*3 shallots, minced fine*
*6 cups chicken broth*
*1 teaspoon lemon juice*
*1/2 teaspoon salt*

> Heat butter in a large saucepan. Sauté shallots and mushrooms over medium heat for 7-10 minutes or until they are soft and have given up their liquor.
> Add chicken broth. Cook slowly for 30 minutes.
> Purée in blender and season with salt and lemon juice to taste.
> Serve hot.

# Cauliflower Soup

In the past, many recipes for cream soups called for the addition of heavy cream or half and half. I have had excellent results using more vegetables and eliminating the high calorie and high fat cream.

---

*2 ribs celery, chopped, and a few tops too*
*1 medium onion, finely chopped*
*3 Tablespoons butter*
*1 large head cauliflower*
*4 cups chicken broth*
*2 cups milk*

---

> In a large saucepan, sauté celery and onion in butter until lightly browned and soft.
> Cut cauliflower head into small pieces. Use all of the head, but not the leaves. Add to the pan with the onion.
> Cover with chicken broth and simmer until cauliflower is very soft.
> Purée in blender until smooth.
> Add milk and reheat. Season to taste with salt and pepper.
> Serve warm or cold with a grating of fresh nutmeg.

The cauliflower soup recipe can be used as the basis for almost any vegetable soup. Simply substitute broccoli, spinach, sorrel or pumpkin for the cauliflower. I would add a touch of additional flavoring for seasoning. Dill goes well in broccoli soup, a little lemon juice works well with spinach or sorrel and nutmeg is great in pumpkin soup. I like to make the pumpkin soup at Halloween with our leftover Jack-O-Lantern. This works well as long as you don't leave your pumpkin out too long or allow it to get too dirty.

-Susan

Presentation is important. Whether you are serving a picnic, a formal dinner or a party brunch, keep in mind that your guests, and you, will see and smell the dish before you taste it. Colorful dishes make an important first impression on the palate.

-Susan

When making sandwiches, always keep your mind open to interesting containers. Just switching to a different bread or a roll can often make the difference between an interesting sandwich and a boring one.

# Armenian Cracker Bread Sandwich Rolls

This is a lunch recipe that makes a good snack or hors d' oeuvres. Vegetarians will find it works well with eggs substituted for the beef.

*a large round Armenian cracker bread*
*1 - 3 ounce package of cream cheese, beaten until*
    *light and fluffy*
*1 Tablespoon prepared horseradish*
*1/4 teaspoon pepper*
*1 Tablespoon milk*
*1/2 pound thinly sliced roast beef*
*1 cup alfalfa sprouts*
*2 medium tomatoes, very thinly sliced*

>Soften cracker bread by holding it under a light spray of cold water for about 10 seconds on each side, or until well moistened, but not soggy. Place between clean, damp towels and let stand until soft and pliable. If there are still some crisp spots, sprinkle additional water over them.
>Mix cream cheese, horseradish and pepper. Stir in milk so cheese will spread easily. Spread the round of cracker bread with cheese mixture. Top with roast beef, sprouts and tomato slices.
>Roll up tightly and wrap in damp towel. Slice just prior to serving.

# Flank Steak Pita Pockets

*1 flank steak*
*1 cup olive oil*
*1/2 cup soy sauce*
*1 onion, chopped*
*2 garlic cloves*
*3 Tablespoons vinegar*
*2 Tablespoons honey*
*pita bread pockets*
*tomato slices*
*alfalfa sprouts*

> Mix all of the ingredients except steak in a blender.
> Marinate steak in sauce at least 3 hours or overnight.
> Grill on hot grill 5-6 minutes per side.
> Serve in pita bread pockets with mustard, tomato slices and sprouts.

Makes 4 well-filled pockets.

# Savory Crisps

This can be used instead of crackers with any cheese or spread. Served with fruits and cheese, it is the simplest, most basic of lunch menus. If you sprinkle these with parmesan cheese before baking, they are a wonderful accompaniment for a bowl of soup. At Turtleback, we serve the Smoked Salmon Appetizer on page 66 with these little crisps.

*1 loaf whole grain bread*
*1/4 pound butter*

At home we serve flank steak marinated and barbecued. This recipe works great with chicken too.

-Susan

A marinade is a liquid that seasons and tenderizes meats. It was originally used by sailors to preserve fish. The word comes from the French, meaning "to pickle in brine." Before marinades were used, salt alone was used as a preservative. A basic marinade consists of two parts oil, one part vinegar, one onion or garlic and seasonings, herbs and spices to taste.

*1 teaspoon savory*
*1 teaspoon sweet basil*
*2 teaspoon finely minced chives*

> Preheat oven to 350°.
> Remove crusts from bread. Cut bread in half on the diagonal.
> Blend butter and herbs and spread on one side of the bread.
> Bake butter side up for about 30 minutes.

# Smoked Salmon Appetizer

Even though this dish is chilled, it is served at room temperature. This makes it a good buffet dish or something to serve when everyone is not eating at the same time. I also recommend this dish for a romantic picnic. It sets an elegant mood, especially if you take along fresh flowers, a white tablecloth and real wine glasses.

*12 ounces smoked salmon*
*1/3 cup minced red onion*
*2 Tablespoons capers, drained*
*3 Tablespoons Vodka*
*1 Tablespoon fresh dill (or 1 1/2 teaspoons dried)*
*1/2 teaspoon ground black pepper, or to taste*
*1 Tablespoon fresh lemon juice*
*1/2 teaspoon minced lemon rind*

---

When serving fruit and cheese be aware of the combining of flavors. Apples are tasty with cheddar cubes, pears are lovely with a young Brie or Camembert. Grapes go well with jack, Jarlsberg or Gruyère.

-Susan

When serving fruit, dip each slice in a water and lemon juice mixture to prevent discoloration.

**To eat is human
To digest divine.
...Mark Twain**

>Bone the smoked salmon and mince.
>Place salmon in a bowl and stir in the remaining ingredients.
>Chill for at least one hour, but let sit at room temperature for about 15 minutes before serving. Serve with savory crisps.

# Holiday Green Sauce

I like to take this dip on a picnic with a basket of fresh vegetables and cookies for dessert. It is easy to prepare, makes a good potluck carry along or a wonderful hors d' oeuvres.

---

*2 cups mayonnaise*
*1/3 cup minced parsley*
*1/3 minced scallions*
*1/3 minced spinach leaves (spines removed)*
*1/3 cup sour cream*
*2 Tablespoon fresh lemon juice*
*2 Tablespoon onion*
*dash Worcestershire*

---

>Whirl everything in a blender or a food processor. Chill.
>Serve in hollowed out red cabbage on a bed of curly leafed lettuce in a festive basket. Surround with assorted raw vegetables; carrot sticks, bell pepper slices, cauliflower florets, zucchini spears, cherry tomatoes, mushrooms, radishes and/or celery sticks.

### Recipe for candied flowers

---

*1 1/2 cups sugar*
*1/2 cup water*
*fresh edible petals*
*tweezers*
*food coloring (optional)*

---

Make a syrup of 1 cup sugar and 1/2 cup water. Boil until it spins a thread. Cool to room temperature. Gently wash and dry petals (whole flowers may also be used). Using the tweezers, dip the petals into the syrup. Shake off any excess and dip into the remaining sugar. Place on waxed paper to dry.

You may also color the sugar the same color as the flower, using food coloring. Allow the mixture to dry thoroughly, stirring occasionaly, before use.

**Best Flowers for Candy**
Rose petals
Gardenia Petals
Mint Leaves
Borage
Violets
Lilacs
Orange Blossoms
Lemon or Lime Blossoms

Pack the supplies you will need last at the bottom of your picnic basket and things you will need first on the top. This way your picnic can unpack in its natural sequence.

When wrapping foods to be eaten later, keep in mind that aluminum foil will stay in place better than plastic wrap, is recyclable and has better insulating properties. You also might want to label foods for easy identification.

# Chicken Pacifica

Because it can be served cold, this is a favorite picnic dish. It also makes a great appetizer.

*2 packages chicken wing drummettes*
*1/2 cup brown sugar*
*1 cube butter*
*1 cup soy sauce*
*3/4 cup water*
*1 teaspoon dry mustard*

>Mix all ingredients except chicken in a saucepan and heat until blended. Cool.
>Add chicken to cooled sauce. Marinate 2 or more hours, turning occasionally.
>Bake in sauce at 350° for 1 hour. Drain.
>Serve hot or cold.
Serves 12 as an appetizer.

# Artichoke Frittata

Even though it is made with eggs, this dish serves well at room temperature.

*12 ounces marinated artichoke bottoms or hearts*
*1 medium onion, chopped*
*2 cloves garlic, minced*
*4 eggs*
*1/2 cup fine, dry bread crumbs*
*1/2 teaspoon salt*
*1/4 teaspoon oregano*
*1/4 teaspoon pepper*
*1/8 teaspoon cayenne*
*2 cups shredded sharp cheddar cheese*
*2 Tablespoons minced parsley*

>Preheat oven to 325°.
>Drain marinade from the artichokes into a skillet. Set the artichokes aside. Add onion and garlic to the skillet and sauté until onion is limp, about 5 minutes.
>In a bowl, beat eggs with a fork. Mix in crumbs, salt, pepper, cayenne and oregano.
>Stir in cheese, parsley, artichokes and the onion/garlic mixture.
>Turn into a buttered 9 inch x 13 inch baking dish. Bake at 325° for about 30 minutes or until set. Let cool in the pan.
>After cooled, cut into bite size squares.
Serves 12 as an appetizer.

**Carnation Vinegar**
Gently but thoroughly wash 2 Carnations. Hold the flower and pull the petals en masse from the stem. Clip off the heels. Place petals in a pint jar. Cover with a good cider vinegar and let the mixture stand for 10 days. Strain before use. This is especially good on fruit salads.

# Wild Rice Salad

This recipe can be made with any type of rice, adjusting to yields. Orzo also works well.

*2 cups water*
*1 cup wild rice*
*1 1/2 cups chicken broth*
*1 clove garlic, peeled but left whole*
*1 bunch scallions, chopped using some of tops*
*3 Tablespoons butter*
*1/2 pound chopped mushrooms*
*3 strips of lean bacon, fried and diced*
*1/2 cup chopped olives, green or black*
*3 Tablespoons capers, less with green olives*
*1/3 cup olive oil*
*3 Tablespoons tarragon wine vinegar*
*1/2 teaspoon margoram*
*1/2 cup sliced celery*
*1/2 cup chopped walnuts*
*salt and pepper to taste*

Wild rice is expensive, but should give a yield of four cups of cooked rice for one cup of uncooked rice. Most other rices will usually yield two cups cooked rice for one cup uncooked rice.

-Susan

To renew old apple trees, use fresh made lime from the kiln. Slake it well with water and go over the tree thoroughly with a large stiff brush. The outer bark will fall off, insects and moss will be destroyed and a new, smooth healthy bark will form.

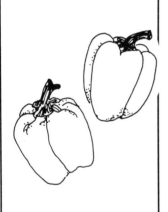

> Soak rice in water overnight. Drain. Rinse, then simmer in chicken broth with garlic clove until all liquid is absorbed and the rice is dry but fluffy. Discard garlic.
> In a medium skillet, melt 3 Tablespoons butter and sauté scallions over low heat until soft. Add mushrooms, increase heat and stir until mushrooms begin to soften, but are still firm.
> Remove from heat and add to rice along with remaining ingredients.
> Toss well. Taste for salt and pepper and chill overnight. Mix well before serving.

Serves 6.

# Tuna Eggplant Salad

This is an exceptional dish for hot weather. I like to serve it with French bread and Chardonnay.

1 eggplant, unpeeled but cut into cubes
3 cloves garlic, mashed
6 Tablespoons olive oil
1 - 6 1/2 ounce can water packed white tuna,
1 cup sliced olives, green or black (optional)
1/2 cup sunflower seeds
10 cherry tomatoes
1 red pepper, diced
1 medium red onion, chopped
2 ribs celery, diced
3/4 cup yogurt
1/2 cup mayonnaise
1 teaspoon oregano
1 teaspoon basil
salt and pepper

>Sprinkle eggplant with 1 teaspoon salt and let it drain for an hour in a colander.

>Drain and flake tuna.

>Sauté half of the eggplant and half of the minced garlic in 3 Tablespoons olive oil until brown, stirring often. This will take about 7 minutes. Set aside in a bowl and repeat with remaining eggplant, garlic and the remaining Tablespoons of olive oil.

>Remove eggplant with slotted spoon and combine both batches with remaining ingredients,except yogurt, mayonnaise and herbs. Chill at least 3 hours.

>Before serving, mix the yogurt, mayonnaise, oregano and basil to make dressing.

>Fold dressing into tuna-eggplant mixture.

>Season to taste. Serve on a bed of lettuce.

Serves 4.

## Pasta Primavera Salad

*1 bunch broccoli florets*
*1 bunch cauliflorets*
*1 zucchini sliced*
*1 summer squash, cubed*
*1 cup green beans, cut*
*1/2 cup peas*
*1 pound vermicelli*
*2 Tablespoons butter*
*2 cloves garlic, minced*
*1 bunch scallions, chopped*
*1 cup mushrooms, thinly sliced*
*1/4 cup parsely, chopped*
*2 Tablespoons fresh basil, chopped*
*2 cups cherry tomatoes, cut into halves*
*oil and vinegar dressing*

Will you teach your children what we have taught our children? That the earth is our mother? What befalls the earth, befalls all the sons of the earth.

This we know: The earth does not belong to man, man belongs to the earth... Man did not weave the web of life, he is merely a strand in it. Whatever he does to the web, he does to himself.

. . . Chief Seattle

**Distilled Vinegar,** probably the most common household variety, is harsh and highly acidic, invaluable for pickling, but less useful for salads.

**Cider Vinegar** tastes unmistakably of its apple origins. Its flavor can overpower all but the strongest oils.

**Rice Vinegars** are light, pleasant and mild, good with delicate greens and quiet oils.

**Balsamic Vinegar** is made from grape must. A wonderful, red-brown, semisweet vinegar, it deserves a place on your shelf.

**Herb Vinegars** are very popular now. The only difficulty with them is that they predetermine the vinegar/herb combination in the night's salad.

**Fruit Vinegars** are actually revivals. Great for cooking fish and chicken.

>Steam each of the vegetables separately until barely tender, 1 - 2 minutes each.
>After cooking, plunge into cold water to stop the cooking process. The vegetables should be crisp. Refrigerate in plastic bags.
>Cook vermicelli al dente. Rinse under cold water and drain. Set aside.
>Sauté garlic and scallions in butter until limp, but not colored.
>Add mushrooms and stir well to coat. Mushrooms should be slightly limp.
>Mix mushrooms, garlic and scallions with vegetables and pasta.
>Add parsley, basil and tomatoes. Combine and chill.
>Just before serving, add dressing and toss.
Serves 4 to 6.

# Favorite Dressing

*juice of one lemon*
*3 Tablespoons white wine vinegar*
*pinch of thyme*
*salt and pepper to taste*
*up to 3/4 cup of salad or olive oil*

>Blend together all ingredients except oil.
>Add oil to personal preference.

# Crêpe Filling

I like to make chicken or seafood crêpes for lunch. When served with a salad they make a complete meal. Basic crêpe recipe is on pg. 29.

*1/4 cup butter*
*1/4 cup flour*
*1 cup milk*
*1/2 cup chicken broth*
*1/2 cup sherry*
*1/4 cup grated Parmesan cheese*
*2 Tablespoons shredded raw milk cheddar or swiss*
*nutmeg, cayenne pepper and salt to taste*
*1 1/2 pounds, crabmeat, shrimp or cubed chicken*

>In a saucepan melt the butter and stir in the flour.
>Whisk in the milk and chicken broth and cook until thickened.
>Add sherry, cheeses, nutmeg, pepper and salt. Heat until cheeses melt and remove from heat. At this point, the sauce can be refrigerated.
>When you are ready to fill your crêpes, make enough crêpes so that each person will have two.
>Cook the crabmeat, shrimp or chicken for the filling. Mix half of the sauce with your choice of filling.
>Preheat oven to 350°.
>Spoon a portion of the filling down the center of each crêpe and fold the sides into the center. Place filled crêpes in an oven proof dish, folded side down. Cover with the remaining sauce and sprinkle with Parmesan cheese, if desired. Put into oven at 350° until heated thoroughly.

Serves 8.

**Other additions to salad dressings:**

Dijon mustard in small amounts adds a savory spicy depth.

Citrus can replace all or part of the vinegar with excellent results.

Cream or yogurt can add substance to a dressing.

**As a member of an escorted tour, you don't even have to know the Matterhorn isn't a tuba.**

...Temple Fielding

# Flower Cuisine

Whenever possible, use garden grown flowers, they offer the greatest fragrance and taste. As a general rule, flowers should be gathered in early morning, washed and refrigerated until used. Flowers which are to be dried, however, should be picked at midday when they are free from moisture. Always wash flowers gently but thoroughly before use.

**Borage** - Clusters of small, blue, star-shaped flowers with a rough gray foliage. Flourishes in ordinary soil, very easily grown and a great attracter of bees. Honeyed cucumber taste, a beautiful garnish.

**Carnation** - Large, originally a pale pink in color, now deep red. Commonly used in wines and the liqueur Chartreuse. Clovelike in flavor and fragrance.

**Chrysanthemum** - Large, bold, yellow with heavy petals. Originated in China 500 B.C. Aromatic piquant flavor, best in soups and salads.

**Dandelion** - Small yellow flowers, dark green leaves. Originated in Greece, Native Americans used it as a medicinal. Young leaves can be cooked and served like spinach, made into a salad, or boiled into tea.

**Gardenia** - Soft, delicate white flowers. Grown in warm climates. Vivid, sweet fragrance. Good for candied flowers.

**Gladiolus** - Many colored varieties, sword-like leaves. Similar to lettuce in flavor, good in salads, beautiful as a garnish.

**Lavender** - Small, violet flowers, of the mint family, very sweet aroma. Commonly used by herbalists; good in soups, salads, teas.

**Marigold** - Large, golden flower with many petals. Very hardy, easy to grow. Mild pleasant, peppery flavor. Commonly used as a flavoring to baked goods and for coloring.

**Nasturtium** - Variety of colors. Originated in Peru. Easy to grow, but needs sun. Light peppery flavor similar to cress. Good for salads and garnishes.

**Pansy** - Deep hues, velvety, face-like flower. Has no distinctive flavor. Best as a garnish.

**Rose** - Use the petals only. High in vitamin C. Good for a large variety of uses including teas, jelly, candy, salads, garnish.

**Violet** - Small, fragrant, white, blue, purple or yellow petals. Readily gives up color and flavor when boiled. High in vitamin C. Good in salads, teas and as a garnish.

If the environment is the meat and potatoes of a place, then the people who live there are the seasonings. Unfortunately, tourists often do not notice the residents of a community. They admire the quaint gift shop, how clean the beach is, or the chummy atmosphere in the café at lunch, but do not give much thought to the people who create and flavor these spots.

Without realizing it, tourists often are drawn to a place by the spirit of the locals, people they rarely bother to know. Travelers, on the other hand, are aware that local residents have as much to offer a visitor as the land itself. Travelers wonder how someone can visit a place and not notice the people who live there. We liken it to dating a girl because she is beautiful, but not talking to her because what she thinks does not interest you.

When you travel to a new area, you have a date with everyone who lives there. Orcas is certainly an attractive companion but, if you look beneath the surface, you will find it is filled with character as well. If the island is a great place to visit, the residents make it that way. They are the ones who work to insure that the island retains its distinctive personality. They are not the clean up crew or entertainment operators, but the people whose home you are visiting. Their personalities create the charm visitors so admire.

Among the first residents most visitors discover, usually without ever meeting them, are the Arnts, Pat and Charlie. Charlie is a retired cowboy actor who has lived on Orcas since 1947. Most locals know the Arnts by their robust character, their children, who are also prominent island citizens, and the fact that Charlie has served as the parade master for the annual 4th of July wing ding.

Visitors know the Arnts by their cattle. Coming into town from the ferry landing, with Crow Valley on your left, you will spy another beautiful, lush valley on your right. Mount Constitution is the backdrop and the Arnt's cattle, striking white Charolais, are the fixtures. A red, white and blue, hand painted sign beside the road informs you of the breed. Evidently many people ask and Charlie wants to be helpful. But the Arnts are just two of many locals who influence your stay.

Lynn Roberts is not an actor, past or present. When you first meet him, you probably will notice his salt and pepper hair, his large eye glasses and his soft spoken manner. He is a down to earth man. For many years he has been the island's appliance repairman. You may pass him on the road as he drives by in his antiquated beige Chevy van. He is an active local businessman. You may read one of his thought provoking letters to the editor in the newspaper, The Island's Sounder.

Lynn thinks that community involvement is essential to good government, that the people who live in an area have a right and a responsibility to govern themselves and determine their own future. For that reason, he is one of the organizers of the monthly town meetings. Many of the decisions regarding community standards are presented or debated at these meetings. His efforts are to inform the populace and encourage island residents to take part in their government.

When you first meet Michael Sky, you might think he has a lot in common with Lynn. Michael is involved in local policy shaping as well. He attends the town meetings and publishes a quarterly newsletter devoted to informing the reader on environmental issues. He also is a driving force behind OPAL, a land trust created to provide affordable low income housing as well as help control local land speculation. But, in contrast to Lynn's livelihood, Michael earns much of his living as a fire walker and has published a couple of books on the subject. Michael is not heavy into bells and feathers, but a serious, well educated man who believes strongly in the power of the mind.

Cy Fraser shares Lynn and Michael's view of planning and control at a local level. He donates large amounts of his time to the Eastsound Planning Commission. You might find him around town, talking to residents about where they think the next street should go, or you might find him cooking at his restaurant, Bilbo's. A Mexican restaurant that has been praised in many publications, Bilbo's dining reflects the island's spirit. Everything is fresh, locally grown when possible, and the atmosphere is relaxed and festive. Even though Cy's business is partially supported by tourists, he does not believe in promotional tourism. "Beauty," he says, "is best discovered, not advertised."

Across the street from Bilbo's is Teezer's, a great place for lunch or homemade cookies. Teezer's is owned by Carolyn and Mark Bledsoe, but the name comes from the fact that Carolyn and her sisters; Lisa, Sandie and Louise, all began life as Ortizes. Of Mexican heritage, all the sisters have worked at Bilbo's at one time or another. Carolyn is an active volunteer in the school. In past years, she has been among the driving forces for the school's annual Holiday Fair, a major fun and fund raiser. The fair is organized by the Orcas Island Education Foundation, a non-profit organization.

The impetus behind the Orcas Island Education Foundation is Kathy Youngren. Kathy also serves on the district school-board. The Youngrens; Kathy, Jim ,and sons Brent, Eric and Andrew operate a non-profit salmon enhancement project on their property. Jim also began and supports Chick and Egg Production, a major funder of the Children's Trust Foundation. The Trust Foundation is a child abuse prevention organization based in Seattle. Chick and Egg Productions produces hand-crafted wooden furniture for children and adults. The young fir poles used in this furniture are cut on Orcas Island and sent to Seattle. The organization's name comes from the idea that child abuse is a cycle, that abused children often grow up to be abusive parents.

The McKay's family business is oysters, raised on Crescent

Beach and shipped to many restaurants across the country. These oysters are so delicious that they are touted by many of those restaurants as being from Crescent Beach. Todd and mom, Erlene, ran the business while his brother Jeff served for four years as a county commissioner. But now, Todd and his wife, Jill, are away at college, so Jeff and mom do much of the work.

The McKays are very patient with the people who walk past the unobtrusive "no trespassing" signs and onto their private beach. The beach is one of the most beautiful scenic places on the island and many visitors are so enthralled that they do not see the signs. They also do not realize they are tromping on the McKay's livelihood, oyster beds. But just as interesting a sight is across the street and up the hill. There you will pass the McKay's house, the yard filled with big horned mountain sheep and llamas. We are told the llamas are South American, not the Oriental variety, and that they love the heat, despite speculation otherwise.

This list of residents, by no means, describes the breadth of Orcas Island character. There are many other examples of what make the island a wonderful place to be.

There are many people with hidden talents in all communities. They quietly pick up litter on the roadway, go out of their way to be helpful to visitors, or donate their time and money to charities. What these people and Orcas Island residents have in common is that they love where they live. They love it enough that they have shaped their lives around supporting local standards. But they have done it in style, maintaining their individuality. That is what feeds all communities. Individuals, as well as natural scenic beauty, are an area's treasures. That is what feeds a community and makes it unique.

My personal preference in cookbooks is for those which provide me with menus. Most cookbook authors, having made the dish several times, have experimented with the flavors and textures that surround a dish. I appreciate the suggestions about what they feel is the best possible combination. Also I enjoy the opportunity to peak inside their heads and have a chance to see their preferences. Knowing their tastes better, I understand more what they intended the dish to be.

With that in mind, I have provided menus in this section. These menus are prepared for four people unless otherwise noted. Page numbers are given for convenience.

## Crown Roast of Pork with Stuffing

**Crown Roast of Pork Dinner**
Mushroom Soup - page 62.
Crown Roast of Pork with Mustard Sauce
Wild Rice and Cranberry Stuffing
Spinach or Chard with Tomato and Garlic
Green Salad
Ice Cream Torte - page 117.

*1 crown roast of pork*

>Preheat oven to 350°.
>Trim roast well. Cover the bone ends with foil. Fit another piece of foil under the roast so that the stuffing does not fall out.
>Place in roasting pan and roast in the oven for 20 minutes, per pound.
>One hour before the roast is done, pile stuffing in the center of the roast. Put it back in the oven to continue roasting. After 30 minutes, cover the stuffing with foil so it does not get too brown.

This dish is a favorite at my house and especially nice for holidays and formal dining occasions. It creates a knockout impression and appeals to a wide variety of palates.
-Susan

> To serve, place roast on serving platter, leaing foil underneath the roast, but re-moving foil covers on the bone ends. Serve with mustard sauce.

# Wild Rice and Cranberry Stuffing

Stuffing can be made the day before and refrigerated until needed.
-Susan

4 cups wild rice, cooked according to package directions
2 cups raw cranberries, coarsely chopped
1/2 cup butter, melted
2 Tablespoons onion, finely chopped
1 teaspoon salt
3 Tablespoons sugar
1/2 teaspoon marjoram
1 clove garlic, minced
1/2 teaspoon mace
1/2 teaspoon thyme
1/2 teaspoon dill
1/2 teaspoon pepper

> Sauté onion in butter for two minutes or until tender.
> Add seasoning and stir until well blended. Cook for two more minutes.
> Stir in remaining ingredients and cook until thoroughly heated, about 10 minutes.
> Let cool.

Although the French are known for their butter laden and cheese filled dishes, they have a lower heart disease rate than Americans, who eat less butter and cheese annually. Baffled experts have purposed several possible explanations for this. Some attribute the healthy French heart to the low stress life style they enjoy. Others think it may be the result of consuming wine with their meals.

"Viva la France!" the response of Orcas Island resident Carol Wright after being informed of the above.

# Mustard Sauce

This sauce is also good with beef or lamb.

*4 Tablespoons pan drippings or butter*
*3 Tablespoons flour*
*1 cup dry white wine*
*1/2 cup chicken or beef broth*
*1/4 cup whipping cream*
*3 Tablespoons dijon mustard*
*1 teaspoon dry mustard*
*salt*
*pepper*

> In a large saucepan, cook flour in the drippings or butter over low heat until lightly colored, about 3 minutes.
> Add wine and broth and cook for 5 minutes or until thickened.
> Add cream and mustard. Cook very slowly for 2 more minutes. Season to taste.
> Serve warm with roast.

# Spinach with Garlic and Tomato

*1 large bunch fresh spinach or chard*
*2 cloves minced garlic*
*1 can solid packed tomatoes or stewed tomatoes*

> Wash and remove stems, chop the spinach or chard. Put in a large pot.
> Add garlic and tomatoes. Heat slowly and thoroughly.
> Serve with a slotted spoon so the vegetable is not soupy.

When roasting meat, allow the meat to remain uncovered to retain its juices. If a rich gravy is desired, place meat in a covered pan or dish.

If you haven't the strength to impose your own terms upon life, you must accept the terms that it offers you.
... T. S. Eliot

Chard may be substituted in any recipe calling for spinach.

-Susan

## Lamb Dinner Menu

Tomato Toasts
Cauliflower Soup - page 63
Butterflied Leg of Lamb with
    Cumberland Sauce
Apple Chutney
Kate's Rice
Spinach Timbale
Green Salad
Chocolate Mousse - page 115

You can tell when steaks and chops are cooked by the appearance of small drops of blood on the uncooked side of the meat. At that point turn the meat and wait again for the juice to appear in small droplets which is a signal that the meat is cooked. Do not use a fork to turn the meat. Use tongs, or a firm wide spatula. If the meat is pricked with the tines of a fork, juices will be lost.

# Tomato Toasts

*12 tomato slices*
*12 thinly sliced pieces of French bread*
*1 cup mayonnaise*
*2 garlic cloves, minced*

>Mix mayonnaise with minced garlic.
>Put one tomato slice on each slice of bread,
    top with a dollop of garlic mayonnaise.
>Broil until mayonnaise is lightly browned.
>Serve hot.

# Butterflied Leg of Lamb

*1 leg of lamb, boned*
*1 cup olive oil*
*1/4 cup dry Vermouth*
*1 Tablespoon oregano*
*2 cloves garlic, peeled and sliced*

1 onion, peeled and cut into eighths
1 dozen peppercorns

---

> Mix all the ingredients in a large bowl except for the lamb.
> Trim most of the fat from the lamb and marinate in the mixture for at least 4 hours. Turn the meat often.
> Barbecue over hot coals for 45 minutes or until pink.
> Slice and serve with Cumberland Sauce.

---

# Cumberland Sauce

---

1/2 cup water
1/2 cup port wine
2 Tablespoons red currant jelly
1/2 teaspoon dijon mustard
pinch cayenne
juice of 1 lemon, save the rind
juice of 1 orange, save the rind

---

> Slice and chop rinds of the orange and the lemon. Boil with 1/2 cup water for 5 minutes. Strain and discard rind.
> Add remaining ingredients and boil for 4 minutes. Cool.
> Serve in a sauce dish.

When hamburger stands began cropping up in Rome a few years ago, wine and food writer, Carlo Petrini became concerned about Italy's gastronomic culture. In defense he founded the *Slow Food Foundation*, dedicated to eating slowly and savoring the moment. Based on the principles that fast food is an impoverishment of a culture and that meals are the only time people in most cultures have to meet and talk, *Slow Food* has now mushroomed in membership in 27 countries and has expanded its agenda to encouraging the banning of pesticides and condemning the deforestation of the Amazon for the purpose of raising cattle.

Chutneys are relishes made with fruits and preserved with sugar, vinegar and spices. They originated in medieval times, giving spark to breads and cheeses. Chutneys are also wonderful compliments to meat dishes, adding color and zest to a meal.

Always stir rice with a fork. Using a spoon bruises the grains and makes them sticky.

# Apple Chutney

20 tart apples
3/4 pound raisins
3/4 pound currants
6 ounces chopped citrus peel
1/4 cup crushed hot peppers
1/4 cup chopped fresh ginger root
1/8 cup minced garlic
2 large onions, chopped fine
1/4 cup preserved ginger, chopped fine
3 pounds sugar
1 1/2 quarts vinegar
1/2 Tablespoon ground ginger
1/2 Tablespoon cumin
1/2 Tablespoon nutmeg
10 pint canning jars

> Bring sugar and vinegar to a boil. Add spices and the remainder of the ingredients. Bring to a boil again and cook over a very low heat for 4 to 5 hours, or until quite thick. Stir occasionally.
> Pack in canning jars according to manufacturer's directions.

Yield: 10 pints

# Kate's Rice

1 cup uncooked rice
1/2 cup butter
4 scallions, sliced thinly, tops too
6 mushrooms, sliced
1 Tablespoon oregano

*1 can bouillon*
*2 cups water*

>Preheat oven to 350°.
>Sauté rice in butter until lightly colored.
>Add scallions, mushrooms and oregano. Sauté together for 5 minutes.
>Add bouillon and water. Pour into covered baking dish and bake for 1 hour or until all liquid is absorbed.

**Never eat more than you can lift. ... Miss Piggy**

# Spinach Timbale

*2-3 bunches fresh spinach, cleaned, stemmed, chopped and blanched*
*4 Tablespoons minced shallots*
*3 Tablespoons butter*
*1/3 cup heavy cream*
*freshly ground nutmeg*
*salt*
*pepper*
*3 eggs*

>Preheat oven to 325°.
>Sauté shallots in butter until limp.
>In a food processor with a metal blade, purée the well dried, blanched spinach with the cream. Add nutmeg, salt and pepper to taste. With the motor running, add one egg at a time and blend for about 3 seconds.
>Divide the mixture between six well-buttered 3/4 cup oven-proof molds. Timbale molds work the best, but if you do not have any, use oven-proof custard cups or individual soufflé bowls.
>Cover each mold with a well buttered

Soufflé is a French word meaning "a puff of wind." The term is used in both cooking and ceramics. Without the accent over the "e", it is a medical term. In cooking it refers to any of several baked foods made light and puffy by the addition of beaten egg whites before baking.

square of foil.

>Place the molds in a deep pan filled with water halfway up the sides of the molds.

>Bake for 25-30 minutes, or until a small knife inserted in the center of one of the molds comes out clean.

>Remove from oven and pan of water and let set for 5 minutes.

>Turn upside down on plates and unmold.

---

**English Pub Dinner Menu**
Scotch Eggs
Pickled  Onions
Potted Shrimp
Steak and  Kidney  Pie
Composted  Salad
Pavlova - page 104
Beer

---

To keep eggs from cracking while boiling, make a small pin prick in the large end (this is where the airsac is) before adding it to the water.

# Scotch Eggs

*6 hard boiled eggs, chilled and peeled*
*1 pound bulk sausage*
*Fine bread crumbs, roughly an amount equal to*
*    the sausage*
*1 raw egg*
*1/4 teaspoon anchovy paste*
*olive oil*

---

>Take out 1/4 cup bread crumbs. Mix the remainder with the sausage.

>Add the raw egg and the anchovy paste to the sausage / bread crumb mixture.

>Roll the peeled eggs in plain bread crumbs.

> Carefully encase each egg in the sausage
   mixture, about 1/4-1/2 inch thick.
> Deep fry in medium hot oil for 5-6 minutes.
   Drain well on paper towels.
> Serve with mustard and pickles.

# Homemade Mustard
## (Famous and Secret)

A guest gave Bill this recipe a couple of years
ago to thank him for making her stay so
special. Since that time, I have made this
mustard for the school Holiday Fair and it has
sold out almost before the fair opened.

*8 ounces Coleman's dry mustard*
*1 cup rice wine vinegar*
*6 eggs, beaten*
*1 cup sugar*
*1/2 stick butter*
*canning jars*

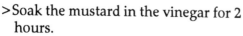

> Soak the mustard in the vinegar for 2
   hours.
> Add the eggs and sugar.
> Cook until mixture reaches a boil, stirring
   occasionally. This scorches very easily, so
   be diligent.
> Remove from heat and add butter. Stir until
   butter melts, then seal in canning jars
   according to manufacturer's directions.
   This keeps in the refrigerator quite well
   and must be refrigerated once opened.

A very entertaining
cooking teacher in
California mixes one
bottle of good English
stout with 4 bottles of
generic beer in a
serving pitcher. It takes
the taste of the
expensive import for a
fraction of the price.
                -Susan

**Seeing is
deceiving. It's
eating that's
believing.**
. . . James Thurber

There ain't no surer way to find out if you like people or hate them than to travel with them.
. . . Mark Twain

**To clarify butter:**
Melt two Tablespoons butter in a small heavy saucepan over low heat until butter melts and white sediment gathers on the bottom of the pan. Pour off clear yellow liquid. Discard sediment. Refrigerate clarified butter and use as needed.

# Pickled Onions

2 *pounds white onions, not pearl onions, but 1*
  *inch boiling onions*
1/2 *cup salt*
1/2 *cup sugar*
1/4 *cup salt*
2 *Tablespoons mixed pickling spice*
6 - 8 *whole cloves of garlic*
10 - 12 *whole peppercorns*
1 *quart malt vinegar*
*wide mouth canning jars or a small crock*

> Put onions in a steamer and steam until they can just barely be pierced. Peel, rinse, put in a bowl with 1/2 cup salt and enough cold water to cover. Let sit overnight.
> The next day, simmer 1/4 cup salt with the remaining ingredients. While the mixture is simmering, pack the onions into jars or a small crock. Pour the spicy vinegar mixture over the onions.
> Refrigerate. These onions will keep 4 to 6 weeks.

# Potted Shrimp

1/4 *pound butter*
1/4 *teaspoon each mace and nutmeg* <u>*or*</u>
  1/2 *teaspoon curry powder*
*pinch cayenne pepper*
2 *cups very small cooked shrimp*
2 *teaspoons lemon juice*
1 *teaspoon onion juice (optional)*
*clarified butter*
*packing jars or 2 - 10 ounce crocks*

>Melt the butter over medium heat. Add mace and nutmeg or curry powder, and cayenne pepper.
>Add shrimp, lemon juice and onion juice. Stir to coat shrimp.
>Carefully pack, so as not to mash shrimp, into crocks or jars. Allow to cool.
>When cool, pour enough clarified butter over the top of the shrimp mixture to completely cover it. Keep refrigerated.
>Serve as spread for crackers or thin pieces of brown bread.

Makes approximately 2 cups.

Henry VIII found the upper or choice part of the loin of beef so good that he knighted it, thus the word sirloin. This is why it is also called a "Baron of Beef."

# Beefsteak and Kidney Pie

*3/4 pound top sirloin of beef, cut into 1 inch cubes*
*1/2 pound lamb or beef kidneys*
*1/4 teaspoon salt*
*1/4 teaspoon pepper*
*1/4 teaspoon paprika*
*1/4 cup all purpose flour*
*1 medium onion, thinly sliced*
*2 Tablespoons shortening*
*2 cups beef stock or 2 cups beef bouillon*
*1 bay leaf*
*4 mushrooms, sliced*
*1 Tablespoon butter*
*1 pie crust*

While browning small pieces of meat, do not allow them to touch. This will retain the meat juices in each piece.

>10 minutes before the pie is to go in the oven, preheat to 450°.
>Trim any fat or membrane from the beef and kidneys. Cut the kidneys into 1/8 inch thick slices.
>Place the salt, pepper, paprika and flour in a paper bag and shake to mix. Add the

Some of the greatest culinary combinations are the simple ones. Be creative, but do not be so busy trying to be different that you hide the flavor of what you are cooking.

-Susan

I do not recommend many vegetable recipes. That is because I believe whole-heartedly in fresh vegetables. If you begin with fresh ingredients, steam them lightly and serve them with a minimum of seasonings and butter, that is the best way to prepare them for flavor and nutrition.

-Susan

beef, kidney and onions and shake until well coated.

>Melt the shortening in a large skillet or dutch oven. Let it get very hot, then add the beef, kidney and onions.

>Sauté, over high heat, stirring constantly, until the meat is brown. Add the stock and bay leaf.

>Reduce the heat to low, cover the skillet and simmer 1 hour or until tender.

>Remove from the heat and discard the bay leaf. Cool. Place the mixture in a 1 1/2 quart baking dish.

>Sauté the sliced mushrooms in butter and put on top of the meat mixture.

>Roll out the pie crust and cover the pie, sealing the edges of the casserole. Cut vents for the steam to escape.

>Bake for 10-15 minutes at 450°, then reduce to 350° and bake an additional 15-20 minutes or until the crust is golden brown.

# Composted Salad

*1/2 pound broccoli*
*1 package frozen green peas*
*1 cup diagonally sliced celery*
*1/2 cup sliced radishes*
*1 cup cherry tomatoes*
*1 cucumber, sliced*
*1 head lettuce*
*salad dressing*

>Cook broccoli in boiling water until just tender. Put under cold running water to stop the cooking action.

>Cook peas until just tender and cool under cold water also.

>Put broccoli, peas and the remaining ingredients, except the lettuce and dressing, in a large bowl. Cover with your favorite dressing and chill for 1 hour.
>When ready to serve, tear the lettuce, mix with the vegetables, toss and serve.

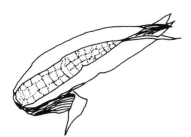

**Fiesta Dinner Menu**
Gazpacho - page 61
Tamale Corn Pie
Corn Tortillas
Orange cake - page 110

# Tamale Corn Pie

This recipe can be made and stored uncooked and covered in the refrigerator or freezer for several days.

*1 chicken, cooked*
*4 large tamales, chicken or chicken and turkey*
*1 can creamed corn*
*1 - 4 ounce can chopped green chilies*
*15 medium or large black olives, cut into thirds*
*1 pound Martin's New York cheese or raw milk*
*    cheddar*

>Preheat oven to 350°.
>Skin chicken and remove meat from bones. Cut meat into chunks.
>Defrost and crush tamales. Put into a large mixing bowl. Add remaining ingredients except cheese. Mix to blend.
>Put 1/3 of the cheese in the bottom of an

This is a fun dinner, but must be made in advance. You will want to make the Tamale Corn and the Gazpacho the day before you plan on serving them. If you are serving guests, this gives you more time with them and less time in the kitchen.

In the Northwest, there is not a large variety of tamales available. I use Garibaldi 11 ounce turkey and chicken tamales, which I found in the frozen food section at Safeway.
                                    -Susan

oven-proof casserole. Add 1/2 tamale mixture. Put another 1/3 cheese over the tamale mixture, then add remaining tamale mixture. Top with remaining cheese.

>Cook at 350° until smooth and bubbly.
>Serve with salsa, sour cream and garnish with cilantro.

---

**Fish Dinner Menu**
Oysters with Leek Purée
Mushroom Soup - page 62
Fresh Fish Parmesan
Scalloped Potatoes
Squash Purée
Strawberry Supreme - page 117

---

Have you ever wondered why most cookbooks contain recipes for rice, noodles and potatoes? This is because many chefs consider these starchs the ideal accompaniment for main courses.

# Oysters with Leek Purée

*1 bunch leeks*
*1/2 cup water*
*1 cup dry white wine*
*1/2 teaspoon salt*
*8 Tablespoons unsalted butter*
*1/4 teaspoon white pepper*
*2 dozen fresh oysters in the shell*
*rock salt as needed*

---

>Clean the leeks. Reserve a few pieces of the dark green portion for garnish. Slice the remainder, using the white and creamy green portion only.
>Simmer leeks, water, wine, salt and 4 Tablespoons of butter in a covered sauce pan for 45 minutes. Leeks should be very soft with

a syrupy glaze. Simmer uncovered for a few minutes to reduce the remaining liquid.

>Purée in a food processor and beat in the remaining 4 Tablespoons of butter, cut into small bits.

>Blanch a few strips of the dark green leek tops in boiling water for 30 seconds, then rinse in cold water to stop the cooking process. Drain, dry and reserve.

>All the above steps may be done a day or two in advance. If you are preparing in advance, refrigerate at this stage.

>Prior to serving, preheat oven to 500°. Open oysters and arrange each on its half shell in rock salt spread on an ovenproof platter or plate. Be careful not to spill any of the oyster liquor.

>Put the leek purée on top of each oyster. Bake for 5 minutes, then put under a broiler for a minute to glaze the purée.

>Garnish each oyster with a piece of the green leek top and serve immediately.

**Sometimes the most urgent and vital thing you can possibly do is take a complete rest.**
**. . . Ashleigh Brilliant**

If you touch the flesh of a scaled fish with your fingers and no impression remains, this is a sign of freshness. A fresh fish has no unpleasant odor and is never slimy. A piece of fresh fish will smell of the sea.

# Fresh Fish Parmesan

*2 pounds red snapper, cod, or other firm white fish*
*1 Tablespoon lemon juice*
*1 Tablespoon Worcestershire sauce*
*1/2 cup flour*
*3 eggs, lightly beaten*
*1 cup freshly grated Parmesan or Romano cheese*
*3 Tablespoons butter*
*2 Tablespoons vegetable oil*

> Cut fish into serving pieces and put into a bowl.
> Sprinkle the Worcestershire sauce and lemon juice over the fillets and turn to coat. Salt and pepper each piece and dredge them in flour.
> Dip fillets into the beaten egg to coat, then cover with a coating of the grated cheese.
> Heat butter and oil in a frying skillet and sauté on each side until brown.
> If the fillets are thick, place the skillet in a 400° oven for 5 minutes to finish cooking.
> Serve immediately.

*Sometimes you have to travel far from home to appreciate how to prepare the local bounty.
. . . Tom Stockley*

When making mashed potatoes use hot milk, or the liquid they were cooked in, cold liquid will make them heavy or soggy. For fluffier mashed potatoes add a pinch of baking soda along with the milk and butter.

## Creamy Scalloped Potatoes

*6 large potatoes*
*1 medium onion, finely chopped*
*3 Tablespoons flour*
*1/4 cup butter*
*3 cups half & half*
*1 teaspoon dried thyme*
*1 Tablespoon parsley, chopped*
*salt*
*pepper*

> Preheat oven to 350°.
> Wash potatoes, leaving skins on. Cut cross-ways into thin slices.
> Butter a 2 quart baking dish. Arrange 1/3 of the potatoes in the bottom of the dish. Top with a dot of butter, a sprinkle of seasonings, a sprinkle of onions and 1 Tablespoon of flour. Alternate a layer of potatoes and a layer of butter, seasonings, flour and onion

until all are used.
>Pour the half & half over the potatoes.
>Cover the dish and bake for 30 minutes.
  Then uncover and bake for 50 minutes
  longer or until potatoes are tender.
>Let stand 5 to 10 minutes before serving.

# Purée of Zucchini
## and Yellow Squash

*3/4 pound zucchini*
*3/4 pound yellow squash*
*1/2 cup chopped onion*
*1 clove garlic, minced*
*3 Tablespoons butter*
*1/2 cup dry white wine*
*1/2 cup water*
*1 teaspoon thyme*
*1 teaspoon oregano*

>Sauté onion and garlic in butter until limp.
  Add chopped zucchini, chopped yellow
  squash, wine and water. Steam until vegetables are tender, adding a little water if
  necessary. Watch carefully as they will
  cook quickly and you do not want to
  scorch the vegetables.
>When soft, put into a food processor with a
  metal blade, juice and all, and process with
  salt, pepper, thyme and oregano. Process
  until almost smooth.
>Serve in individual au gratin dishes.

Steam or stir fry
vegetables whenever
possible to avoid losing
flavor and vitamins. If
you do boil vegetables,
bring the water to a boil
before you drop them
in. Never let vegetables
stand in cold water
before cooking. The less
exposure to air and
water that the
vegetable gets, the
better. Prepare the
vegetables as close to
cooking time as
possible or cook them
whole and slice after
they are cooked.

---

**Mussel Dinner Menu**
Mussels in Cream
Green Salad
Sourdough French Bread - page 43
Fresh Fruit Sorbet - page 118

---

Mussels are very rich, especially when prepared with a wine/cream sauce. This may be offered as the first course of a very fancy dinner or makes a delicious but simple dinner when served with the menu above.

-Susan

Mussels are steamed not only to cook them but to facilitate the opening of the shell.

# Mussels in Cream

*2 cups dry white wine*
*1/2 cups shallots or the white part of scallions, finely chopped*
*8 sprigs parsley*
*1 bay leaf*
*1/4 teaspoon thyme*
*pinch finely ground pepper*
*4 dozen mussels, scrubbed and debearded*
*1 cup heavy cream or half and half*
*1 tablespoon arrowroot for thickening (may be omitted)*

---

>In a large saucepan, boil the wine, shallots, herbs and pepper. Add mussels and cover tightly. Cook until shells open, about 5 minutes. When shells have opened, place the mussels in a large serving bowl and keep warm.

>Strain the cooking liquid through a fine cloth and stir in the cream blended with arrowroot. Cook over high heat three minutes more.

>Ladle the sauce over the mussels. Top with minced parsley and serve immediately.

**Barbecued Hen Menu**
Barbecued Cornish Game Hens
Corn on the Cob
Chard with Garlic and Tomatoes
Green Salad
Favorite Cheesecake - page 108

# Barbecued Cornish Game Hens

My father, because he was both an actor and an olympic athlete, was seen as an authority on health and fitness. He once did an exercise book that included much of his advice and experience on keeping fit. When the book came, my siblings and I looked through it to see what dad was up to now. We found the publisher had included a recipe for "Buster Crabbe's Famous Barbecue Chicken," even though dad, to the best of our knowledge, did not enjoy barbecuing. When asked about it, he agreed that barbecue was not his forté, but added that if he did barbecue, he would like his chicken done this way. I present this recipe in his honor. I miss him.

If you do not have a covered kettle type barbecue, you can roast these in a 375° oven for about the same amount of time.

-Susan

Since game birds are very lean, larding is necessary. Strips of bacon will always enhance the flavor and moistness.

4 game hens
1/2 teaspoon salt
7 slices bacon
2/3 cup minced onion
1/3 pound chopped chicken livers
1/2 cup butter. melted
4 slices of homestyle bread, processed into crumbs
1/2 teaspoon sage
1/4 teaspoon pepper

Corn on the Cob is great roasted in the oven, rather than boiling it. Just butter each piece and cover it with foil, then roast at 350° for about 15 - 20 minutes. It retains more of the vitamins and flavor when prepared this way.

Beets may also be prepared in the same manner, but will require an hour to cook.

As a side dish, onions are also good this way. Peel the onion and make an X on the top and bottom with a knife so that the onion does not rupture. Wrap in foil and cook for 45 minutes at 350°. You will get the best flavor with a sweet onion such as Walla Walla or Vidalia.

-Susan

>Begin heating the charcoal to a grey red. While it is heating, prepare the game hens.

>Clean and dry hens. Sprinkle salt into the cavity of each hen.

>Dice 3 slices of bacon and cook them with the onion and liver in 1/4 cup butter until the onion is tender and the livers lose their color.

>Add bread crumbs, 1/2 teaspoon salt, sage and pepper. Stir until well blended.

>Stuff hens with the mixture and sew or skewer openings closed. Wrap a slice of bacon around each breast and secure with a wooden toothpick. Brush with remaining 1/4 cup of butter.

>After the coals begin to glow, put a drip pan made of foil under the middle of the grill on the coals to catch the grease. Replace the grill and put the birds over the drip pan in a circle, leaving the center of the grill open.

>Cook about 45 - 60 minutes covered or until brown and well done.

# Salad

We always have our salad in the European manner, after the main course. I am not totally sure why. Perhaps we felt a longing for Europe one evening, or more likely I forgot to wash the lettuce and dinner was ready. Whatever the reason, it seems to wind the dinner down. It gives us and our guests a respite during the festive atmosphere of a meal  and a chance to gear up for dessert.

I like to use a mixture of different greens in my salads; salad bowl lettuce, endive, sprouts, butter lettuce, all in combination. I do not have a set proportion, just whatever looks good at the market. We add sliced tomatoes, mushrooms, radishes, celery, carrots, sometimes a crumbling of goat's cheese.

I also dress the salad lightly, in the bowl, before serving. One of my pet peeves is a salad loaded with strong dressing. A good salad does not need all that.

This is a recipe for one of my favorite homemade dressings. It can be stored in the refrigerator if you do not use it all. Always be sure to taste every dressing you make to be certain you have not added too much vinegar.

## Caper Dressing

*1 Tablespoon capers*
*1 heaping teaspoon dijon mustard*
*pinch salt*
*pinch sugar*
*1/2 teaspoon thyme or oregano*
*4 Tablespoons Balsamic vinegar*
*3/4 cup olive oil or salad oil*

>Mix all ingredients thoroughly in blender.

To make colorful onion rings for garnishing salads, let the rings soak with pickled beets or beet juice. Walnuts or pecans toasted in butter and garlic salt are also a delicious garnish for a salad.

Use salad dressing sparingly; a thin coating is all that is needed.

The proportions for a perfect oil and vinegar dressing are one part vinegar to two parts oil.

When replacing dried herbs with fresh herbs as a general rule use twice the amount. Most fresh herbs will keep well for a few days in the refrigerator if stored in a screw top jar.

**Lasagne Dinner Menu**
Lasagne  Rolls
Marinated   Vegetables
Sourdough French Bread - page 43
Luscious  Lemon  Dessert - page 116

# Lasagne Rolls

## Tomato Béchamel Sauce with Herbs

This recipe serves a lot of people. I make this dish when preparing a party for teenagers or taking food to a pot-luck.

-Susan

1/4 cup butter
1/4 cup flour
3 Tablespoons chopped fresh basil <u>or</u>
   1 Tablespoon dried basil
3/4 teaspoon of fresh thyme <u>or</u>
   1/2 teaspoon dried thyme
generous pinch oregano
2 cups milk
1 cup tomato purée
3 egg yolks
salt and pepper to taste
freshly grated nutmeg
1 Tablespoon butter

When serving a meal that contains fat, plan on a citrus fruit dessert. The fruit cuts the grease and cleanses the  palate.

-Susan

>Melt butter in heavy non-aluminum sauce - pan over low heat until bubbly. Remove from heat and whisk in flour and herbs. Return to heat and cook, stirring constantly for four minutes, being certain that the flour does not brown.

>Whisk in milk and continue cooking until thickened.

>Stir in tomato purée. Remove from heat and cool for five minutes.

>Whisk in egg yolks. Season with salt, pepper and nutmeg.

> Transfer to storage container and plop 1 Tablespoon butter over the top of the sauce and allow it to melt to keep a skin from forming.
> Cover and refrigerate until ready to use.

## Lasagne

---

1/4 cup butter
2 medium onions, finely chopped
3 cloves of garlic, minced
1/2 cup chopped almonds or pinenuts
3 pound fresh spinach, washed and trimmed
1/3 cup raisins
1 pound ricotta cheese, drained
1/2 pound minced Italian salami (may be omitted)
4 scallions, minced
1 egg yolk
3 Tablespoons parsley, minced
3 Tablespoons fresh basil or 1 Tablespoon dried
5 ounces fontinella cheese, shredded
8 ounces Parmesan cheese, grated
3 ounces Swiss or Gruyère chesse, shredded
3/4 pound lasagne noodles

---

> Cook spinach just until wilted, then squeeze dry and chop.
> Cook lasagne noodles according to package directions until al dente, then rinse in cool water, drain and pat dry with paper towels.
> Melt butter in large non-aluminum sauce pan, add onion and cook on low heat, stirring frequently until browned and carmelized, about 25 minutes.
> Add garlic and nuts and cook 1 minute longer.
> Stir in spinach and cook until until dry.
> Remove from heat and season with salt, pepper and nutmeg. Blend in raisins and

5 packages of frozen spinach may be used in this recipe if fresh spinach is unavailable. Thaw the spinach, chop it finely, then squeeze it dry.

- Susan

When cooking pastas be sure to add a little oil to the water. Pastas have a tendency to stick together. If you want to prepare it ahead, when cooked al dente, remove from heat and rinse until cool. Drain and cover with a wet cloth to keep the top from drying out. To reheat, put pasta in a collander and dip into boiling water. Individual servings or the entire batch can be heated and served at your convenience.

A mushroom has no apparant leaves, blossoms or fruits. Indeed it is not a true plant, but a fungus. The mushroom itself is the fruit of the fungus and contains the spores or seeds. Mushrooms are very low in calories. Use mushrooms as soon as possible after buying them. Do not leave them exposed to sun or air. Mushrooms should be stored in the refrigerater in paper bags to keep them from weeping. Removing the skins weakens the structure of the mushroom, so they are best served unpeeled. When sautéing fresh mushrooms, sprinkle with a little lemon juice to prevent discoloration.

let cool.

> Combine ricotta, salami, scallions, egg yolk, parsley, basil, salt and pepper in a bowl and blend.
> In another bowl blend cheeses together.
> Preheat oven to 375°. Butter a 9 inch X 13 inch baking dish and spread a thin layer of the béchamel sauce over the bottom. Whisk the sauce a few times to lighten it before putting it in the bottom of the pan .
> Lay each lasagne noodle out and spread with a thin layer of spinach and ricotta mixture. Roll up jelly roll fashion and set upright in the bottom of the pan.
> Sprinkle with the cheese mixture and pour béchamel sauce over it just before baking.
> Bake 45 to 60 minutes until bubbly and browned. Let cool slightly before serving.

Serves 10.

# Marinated Vegetables

*carrots*
*zucchini*
*broccoli*
*mushrooms*
*caper dressing  (recipe on page 99)*

> Wash all vegetables thoroughly.
> Peel carrots and cut into similar size sticks. Steam or boil until barely tender.
> Separate broccoli into florets and steam or boil until barely tender.
> Cut unpeeled zuchini into sticks and steam or boil until barely tender.
> Slice mushrooms.

>Refrigerate each vegetable separately in a little dressing.

>At serving time arrange the vegetables on a bed of lettuce, alternating them around the plate and piling the mushrooms in the center. Cover with remaining dressing.

## Fun Garnish for Dinner Plates

### Citrus Butterflies

Choose a firm piece of citrus fruit (lemon, lime or orange) that has few seeds. Take a very sharp knife and cut into thin slices. Remove the seeds. Cut a V shaped wedge from the slice. Turn the slice around and cut another wedge making this one larger than the first. Discard the cutout pieces. You should have two triangular shaped pieces, thinly attatched. Place two thin strips of red bell pepper to represent the feelers.

**Favorite Toasts**

May you be granted health, wealth and happiness and the wisdom to enjoy them all.

* * * *

May your memories of the past bring you as much pleasure as your anticipation of the future.

* * * *

May you always have many friends; old ones to help you grow old and new ones to help you stay young.

* * * *

May the celebration of life forever sing in your ears.

**A warm smile is the universal language of kindness.**
... Wm. Arthur Ward

# Washington Wines

The experts say that high quality wines require vines grown in relatively low humidity and well drained ground, both of which can be found in Washington state. Due mostly to the Japanese Current just off-shore, the climate there is mild. Summers are warm and dry, with low precipitation and infrequent cloud cover, perfect wine-growing weather. The state is also blessed with long, warm summer days and cool crisp nights despite its northerly 47° latitude. This is important during the ripening period.

The majority of the 10,000+ acres of premium wine grapes are concentrated in the south-central portion of the state. Several varietals (see below) have produced wines of distinctive quality.

There are no set rules about matching a wine with a particular food. Choosing a wine is like choosing paint for a room. Personal taste is used to coordinate the color with the decor. Wine selection is based on experience and personal preference. When serving more than one wine, just as with paint, start with the lighter wines and finish with the heavier (darker) ones.

**Cabernet Sauvignon** is the major red wine of Washington. Rich and complex, it is the classic Northwest accompaniment to steaks, roasts and heavily seasoned entrées.

**Chardonnay** is the queen of white grapes. Rich and buttery with a crisp acidity, the Chardonnays complement seafoods, poultry and light meats.

The **Merlot** produces a rich red wine that is gentle on the palate. A fast growing varietal it makes a great accompaniment to sharp cheeses and flavorful meats.

The **White Riesling** is also called the **Johannisberg Riesling** in Washington. Wines labeled "White" tend to be sweeter than wines labeled "Johannisberg." Both complement a broad selection from hors d'oeuvres to desserts.

The **Sauvignon Blanc** is excellent with seafood or as an apertif with appetizers. It is also called a Fumé Blanc when aged in oak.

Here are a few of the Washington wines that we recommend to complement recipes in this book.
**The Hogue Cellars** - Fumé Blanc, Cabernet Sauvignon, Merlot
**Chateau Ste. Michelle** - Cabernet Sauvignon, Merlot, Chardonnay
   and Johannisberg Riesling
**Covey Run** - Cabernet Sauvignon, Merlot

All of us have different ideas about what is necessary for good health. For those of us who earn our living in the city, just getting away from our daily work environment can be the first step toward restoring our health and sanity. For those who live in rural areas, a trip to the city might be needed to shake off the effects of cabin fever. We have devoted this chapter to what we feel is a basic component of good health, both physical and mental, the sweets of the palate and the sweets of the soul.

Health experts tell us the most helpful aspect of a vacation is the exposure to different sensory input. Our minds and bodies need pleasant new experiences from time to time to keep us alert, healthy and happy. We believe this so much that we do not use the term vacation when we travel. This word implies to vacate the mind, which is what many of us do in our daily routines, where mindfulness often is not a requirement. Instead we prefer the word holiday. If we do it right, a trip, or even a good meal, is a holiday; a filling of the senses with sounds, tastes, sights, textures, celebration and new perspectives.

There are many ways to take holidays, some big and some small. Travel forces us to discover dormant talents and abilities because we can not fall back on the familiar in strange environments. Orcas Island brought our health to mind because the island has a reputation for being a place of rejuvenation. Testament to the true nature of Orcas is the Healing Arts Center, almost in the center of the island. There one can receive or learn to give a massage, among other therapeutic possibilities.

Probably the biggest part of the healing Orcas Island offers is its rural setting. The constant stimulation of the traffic, people and noise that we find in the city is more of a jolt to the system than a soothing hand. On Orcas, there are no malls, entertainment centers or nightclubs to offer distraction. The term party is most often applied to a potluck barbecue. The locals like it that way. After all, they go to Seattle when they want an adventure. We found Orcas, like many rural destinations, a great place to unplug from the television, the news and the world in general and wrap ourselves in a cocoon of fresh experiences.

But one need not travel to an island to have this experience. There are ways to create this experience in our everyday environment, the most obvious being keeping a promise to ourselves to try new things. This is one reason that we believe in mini-holidays. We have found that when we have the blahs, just going to a new restaurant, or putting together a new dish at home is often enough to pull us out of it. A little new stimulation is sometimes all the body and mind needs to feel the enjoyment of life once again. This can be a new dance step, a walk in the park, a different restaurant or a new recipe. Wherever you live, we recommend you take the time to get away from it all from time to time. Turn the television off, put on your favorite music, let the answering machine take your calls, sip a little wine, and whip up a treat in the kitchen. It will definitely make your stay on planet earth more fun and relaxing. And it might add a few years to your life.

There are sure to be those who protest, but we strongly believe that sweets and desserts are somehow connected to longevity. Desserts in themselves are not dangerous or sinful, despite what you may have been told. It is the quantity in which we eat them that can become disastrous. A health magazine to which we subscribe recently featured an article on the importance of having dessert. The article informed us how dessert can round out the nutrients in a meal, especially when the sweet contains fresh fruit. In small quantities, generally 2 to 4 tablespoons, even really rich desserts like hot fudge sundaes, can keep our sweet tooth at bay and ward off those often regretted binging sprees. Better an ounce of something wonderful, we are told, than a pound of denial and longing or a frenzy of over-indulgence. (Although a friend of mine described these portions as exquisite torture.)

But another important aspect of those special foods and events is that they keep our outlook bright. The evidence is quickly mounting that a lack of stress in our lives is not the optimum condition. Rather than a state of perpetual relaxation, we need lives rich with things we enjoy. People, places, events and foods that please us stimulate our minds and bodies, as well as make staying alive worthwhile. These benefits are strongest, we believe, when we do whatever it is that pleases us in a conscious state of mind. In other words, if you treat yourself to the delicacies of a chocolate mousse, enjoy every bite. Let all your senses take in the experience and savor it for all it's worth. As our parents taught us, anything worth doing is worth doing well. We see no reason why that maxim shouldn't be applied to desserts.

And now, we proudly present, Susan's treats.

## Spiced Cup Cakes

1 cup raisins
2 cups water
1/2 cup shortening
1 3/4 cups flour, sifted
1 cup sugar
1 teaspoon baking soda
pinch salt
1 teaspoon cinnamon
1 teaspoon clove
1 teaspoon allspice
1 teaspoon nutmeg
1 egg, beaten
1/2 cup or more chopped nuts

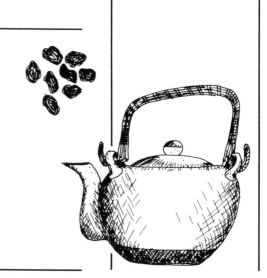

We have all been to potluck's. But have you ever considered an all dessert one? These are especially good over celebrational or holiday times. Add a couple of dessert wines and coffee and you have an instant party.

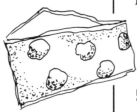

When cutting a cheesecake or any gooey dessert, run warm water over your knife first. The slices will cut cleaner.

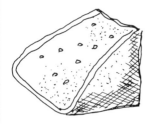

> Boil raisins in water for 10 minutes. Let cool for 5 minutes.
> Preheat oven to 375°. Grease and flour muffin tins or line with paper liners.
> Add shortening to raisins.
> Mix dry ingredients together. Add to raisin mixture.
> Add beaten egg and nuts. Stir to blend.
> Pour into prepared muffin tins. Fill each cup a little over 1/2 full. Bake for 30-40 minutes or until done. Can be frosted with buttercream frosting or served plain.

Makes 12 cupcakes.

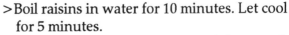

# Favorite Cheesecake

### Crust

---

*1 package graham crackers*
*4 Tablespoons butter*
*1 1/4 Tablespoon sugar*

---

> Preheat oven to 350°.
> Process the above in a food processor with on/off pulses until the crackers are uniform crumbs. Press into the bottom and up the sides of a 10 inch springform pan.
> Bake 10 minutes or until lightly browned. Cool.

### Filling

---

*2- 8 ounce packages cream cheese*
*1/2 cup sugar*

*2 eggs*
*1/2 teaspoon vanilla*

---

>Preheat oven to 375°.
>Process all the filling ingredients in a food processor until the mixture is smooth, about 3 minutes. Scrape down the sides and process again to insure that the mixture is well blended.
>Pour into prepared crust and bake for 25 minutes. Cool 30 minutes.

**Topping**

---

*2 cups sour cream*
*2 Tablespoons sugar*
*1/2 teaspoon vanilla*

---

>Preheat oven to 475°.
>Blend together all ingredients. Cover the cream cheese mixture with the topping.
>Return to the oven and bake for 5 minutes.
>Remove from the oven. Cool, then refrigerate at least 4 hours or overnight.

# Spiced Pound Cake

This is a versatile pound cake. It is good enough to serve plain or it can be dressed up with fresh fruits, sherbets or ice creams.

---

*1 cup butter*
*1 1/2 teaspoon freshly grated nutmeg*
*1/2 teaspoon salt*
*1 2/3 cups sugar*
*5 eggs*
*2 cups flour*

Physical appearance is often a reflection of a person's health. No physical attribute tells more about a person's health than their skin. A nutritious diet, exercise, fresh air and lots of water will to give the skin a healthy glow. Facial masks not only deep clean the skin, but they are soothing as well. Such masks can often be made at home from natural ingredients. One of our favorites is made from crushed almonds. Add a liquid, such as milk, yogurt or water to the almond meal and make a paste. Apply this to a clean face, allow it to dry, then wash it off with cool water. Almond oil is used in making creams, lotions and body oils.

A cake will be less likely to stick to the pan if you put the pan on a wet towel to cool as soon as you remove it from the oven.

A few marigold petals added to bread dough or cake batter will give the resulting baked good a pale yellow color and a wonderful flavor. One tablespoon is generally all that is needed.

> Do not preheat oven, but have ingredients at room temperature.
> Grease and flour tube pan.
> Beat butter, nutmeg and salt with mixer for 5 minutes. Add sugar and beat until fluffy, 2 minutes or more.
> Beat in 4 of the eggs, one at a time.
> Stir in all of the flour and beat again about 3 minutes. Beat in the last egg just until thoroughly mixed.
> Pour batter into a greased pan and place into the cold oven.
> Turn oven on to 300° and bake for 2 hours or until a cake tester comes out clean.
> Cool in pan about 10 minutes. Then turn out onto a wire rack to cool completely.

# Orange Cake

Cake flour makes a lighter cake without sifting.
    -Susan

1 1/4 cups flour plus 1 Tablespoon
2 teaspoons baking powder
1/4 teaspoon baking soda
peel of one orange, only the orange skin, not any of the white
1 cup sugar
3 large eggs, room temperature
1/2 cup butter, room temperature
1/2 cup fresh orange juice
glaze, recipe page 111

> Preheat oven to 375°.
> Grease and flour a 6 1/2 cup bundt pan or ring mold.
> Mix all dry ingredients except sugar in a bowl.
> Place the orange peel in the bowl of the

food processor and chop. Add 1/2 cup sugar and process until very fine. Add the remaining sugar and eggs and process for 1 minute. Scrape the sides of the bowl and process again about 10 seconds.

> Add butter. Process for 1 minute. Scrape down the sides of the bowl and process until fluffy, about 1 minute.
> With the machine running, pour orange juice down feed tube and process until well blended.
> Add flour mixture and process until just blended, about 3-4 pulses.
> Pour batter into prepared pan and spread evenly.
> Bake 20-25 minutes or until cake pulls away from the sides of pan and a tester comes out clean. Watch carefully because this cake is easy to overbake.
> Invert on cooling rack and let cool while you prepare the glaze.

### Glaze

*1/4 cup apricot jam*
*1 Tablespoon lemon juice*
*1 Tablespoon sugar*
*1 Tablespoon rum*

> Boil jam, lemon juice and sugar together until bubbly, about 2 minutes.
> Strain mixture into a bowl.
> Let cool a little and add rum.
> Slowly pour warm glaze over warm cake so the mixture is absorbed.
> Serve slices of cooled cake with the topping of your choice.

**Suggested Toppings:**
vanilla ice cream
whipping cream
yogurt sweetened with
    a little honey
apricot slices
nectarine slices
nasturtiums
borage
fruit purées
creme fraiche
chocolate shavings
melba sauce
favorite liqueur

Pears make a wonderful dessert. Choose either Bartlett, Anjou or Bosc pears. In a pan large enough to hold 6 pears side-by-side, boil 1 3/4 cups of dry red wine,1 cup sugar, 1/4 teaspoon anise seeds, 2 cinnamon sticks and 2 lemon slices. Add pears, reduce heat to medium and simmer until Bartletts are heated and still hold their shape and the Bosc and Anjou can be pierced easily with a fork, about 12-15 minutes. Remove pears with a spoon and reduce cooking liquid to a syrup. Pour over the pears. Serve warm.

Whenever a recipe calls for granulated sugar, consider using bartender's sugar. Its fine texture lends itself well to light desserts. To make your own super fine sugar, process granulated sugar in a food processer until powdery. Make sure the sugar is dry before processing.

Any ripe, sweet fruit can be used instead of kiwis on the Pavlova. My favorites are peaches, raspberries or strawberries. Use your favorite for variety.
-Susan

# Pavlova

Pavlova is an Aussie dessert. Bill homesteaded in Australia for a few years, so this is one of his favorites. This is a natural for us because we often use Hollandaise at the inn. The contrast of flavors and textures in this dish is always interesting.

*4 egg whites, room temperature*
*1/2 teaspoon salt*
*1/4 teaspoon cream of tartar*
*1 cup fine granulated sugar*
*4 teaspoon cornstarch*
*2 teaspoons white wine vinegar*
*1 teaspoon pure vanilla*
*1 cup heavy cream, whipped*
*2-3 kiwis, peeled and sliced*

> Preheat oven to 275°.
> Grease and flour a 10 inch springform cake pan.
> Place egg whites in mixer bowl with salt and cream of tartar. Beat until they hold stiff peaks.
> Add sugar, 1 heaping Tablespoon at a time, beating constantly until mixture is smooth and glossy. This takes 7-10 minutes.
> Beat in cornstarch, vinegar and vanilla.
> Pile gently into cake pan. Pile higher on sides to form a bowl.
> Bake in slow oven, 60 - 90 minutes. Bake until meringue is pale beige and firm. It will pull away from the sides of the pan.
> Whip cream just before serving and pile on Pavlova. Cover top with sliced kiwi.
> Serve at once.

# Stilton or Roquefort Cookies

*2 1/4 cups flour*
*1/2 cup powder sugar*
*1/2 teaspoon salt*
*1/2 teaspoon white pepper*
*1 cup butter*
*1 cup Stilton or Roquefort cheese*
*3 Tablespoons dry sherry*
*1 2/3 cups finely chopped, toasted walnuts*

>Sift together dry ingredients. Cut in butter until mixture resembles corn meal.
>Add cheese and mix until blended.
>Sprinkle with sherry and 1 cup walnuts. Blend well and shape into logs about 9 inches long. Roll logs in remaining walnuts, pressing firmly into dough. Wrap in wax paper and chill well.
>Preheat oven to 400°.
>Cut dough into 1/4 inch slices. Place slices on a lightly greased cookie sheet and bake for 8 minutes or until lightly browned. Cool on wire racks.
>Serve with fruit, cheese and white wine.
Makes 3 dozen cookies.

# Walnut Shortbread

*2 cups soft butter*
*1 cup sugar*
*1 cup walnut pieces*
*2 teaspoons vanilla*
*1/4 teaspoon salt*
*4 cups sifted flour*

Egg whites at room temperature beat up faster and to a larger volume than cold ones. A properly beaten white should triple its volume. Egg whites will not beat up properly if either the bowl or beaters are even slightly moist or greasy.
-Susan

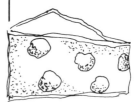

Cheese should always be served at room temperature for the best taste and texture.

Few things are more soothing than a hot cup of herb tea. Camomile tea is a natural relaxer; tea made from rosehips contains a large amount of vitamin C; mint teas aid in digestion and tea made from comfrey is a natural decongestant.

The word cake comes from an old Teutonic word, kaka. The English used the dimunitive form, koekje, to make the word cookie.

The Japanese have been researching a controversial treatment called aromatherapy. This therapy is based on the premise that certain scents can wipe away tension and fatigue and help us to relax. Among the scents that they have found to have relaxation benefits are: basil, its fresh smell has a hot and cold feel to the skin which is very comforting; camomile, used to reduce insomnia and stress; eucalyptus, its camphor like smell calms the nerves; lavender, a gentle pick-me-up; jasmine, known for centuries for its sensual properties.

>Preheat oven to 325°.
>Prepare 15 inch X 10 inch X 1 inch jelly roll pan, lightly grease sides and bottom.
>Grind walnuts to a coarse meal in food processor, blender or food grinder.
>Cream butter and sugar until light and fluffy.
>Beat the nuts, vanilla and salt into butter mixture. Add flour and mix well.
>Spoon the dough into pan and smooth it out to fill pan easily. The dough will not change shape as it cooks so level the top with a spatula so it will cook evenly.
>Bake 40-45 minutes until lightly browned.
>Cool in pan, then cut into bars.
Makes 75 - 1 inch X 2 inch bars.

# Nut Cookies

*1 egg*
*1 cup dark brown sugar*
*5 Tablespoons flour*
*pinch baking soda*
*pinch salt*
*1 cup chopped walnuts*
*1/2 teaspoon vanilla*

>Preheat oven to 325°.
>Beat egg. Stir in brown sugar, flour, soda and salt.
>Add nuts and vanilla.
>Pour into buttered 8 inch X 8 inch pan. Bake 30-40 minutes. Allow to cool in pan.
>Cut into squares.
Makes 16 - 2 inch squares.

# Chewy Chocolate Chip Bars

1/2 cup butter
1/2 cup firmly packed brown sugar
1 cup flour
2 eggs
1 cup firmly packed brown sugar
1 1/2 teaspoon vanilla
2 Tablespoons flour
1 teaspoon baking powder
1/2 teaspoon salt
1 cup finely chopped nuts
1 cup bittersweet chocolate chips

> Preheat oven to 350°.
> Mix the first three ingredients together.
> Pat into bottom of a greased 9 inch X 13 inch pan.
> Bake for 10 minutes. Cool.
> Beat together the remaining ingredients, keeping the chocolate chips aside.
> Spread the mixture over the first layer and sprinkle chocolate chips over the top.
> Bake at 350° for 25 minutes or until lightly browned.
> Cool, then cut into bars.

Makes 24 bars.

# Chocolate - Espresso Mousse

4 ounces semisweet chocolate <u>or</u>
   3/4 cup chocolate chips
1/2 cup butter
1/4 cup strong espresso
6 Tablespoons sugar
3 large eggs

We recommend moderation as opposed to martyrdom when it comes to the question of food and health. As gourmets we realize the importance of well prepared food and drink. As health conscious adults we know the importance of good nutrition. When we entertain we have found that a few simple substitutions will cut calories and fat without sacrificing the festive atmosphere.

For example: Four ounces of Champagne saves 251 calories and 16 grams of fat over an equal amount of egg nog. Many cheese shops now carry gourmet cheeses which can save you many calories over high fat Brie. Pretzels, grilled shrimp, pita wedges and fresh vegetables are also better nutrition choices.

If you do not have an espresso machine, you can use instant espresso.
-Susan

The best way to melt chocolate is over a very low heat in the top of a double boiler over hot water. If you add a little butter when you melt the chocolate, it will help prevent burning the chocolate and also makes it easier to clean the pan afterwards.

**Maturity means reaquiring the seriousness one had as a child at play.
. . . Nietzsche**

> Over low heat in a small heavy saucepan, melt the chocolate with the espresso.
> While chocolate is melting, cut the butter into small pieces and put it in the bowl of a food processor fitted with a metal blade. Process the butter with the sugar until fluffy, about 1 minute.
> Add warm melted chocolate-espresso mixture. Process 15 seconds. Scrape sides of bowl and process for another 20 seconds.
> Add eggs, one at a time, and process for 15 seconds with each egg addition.
> Divide the mousse into individual serving dishes and refrigerate until well chilled, at least 4 hours.

Serves 4-6.

# Luscious Lemon Dessert

When this dessert is finished it is layered with the custard on the bottom and the soufflé on the top. It can be served with a sprinkling of fresh berries as a garnish.

---

*1/2 cup unsalted butter, softened*
*1 1/2 cups sugar*
*6 large eggs, at room temperature*
*2/3 cup fresh lemon juice*
*zest of the lemons used to make the juice, minced*
*2/3 cup flour*
*3 cups half & half*
*1/2 teaspoon salt*

---

> Pre-heat oven to 350°.
> In a food processor with a metal blade, cream together the butter and the sugar

until the mixture is light and fluffy.

> Separate eggs. Add the yolks one at a time to the butter and sugar mixture, beating well after each addition.
> Beat in lemon juice, zest and flour. Stir in half & half and blend until well combined.
> In a separate bowl, beat the egg whites with the salt until they hold soft peaks. Be sure not to over-beat.
> Fold 1/4 of the whites into the lemon mixture until lightened. Then gently fold in the remainder until blended.
> Pour batter into a lightly buttered 9 inch round cake pan. Put this pan into a larger pan and fill the larger pan with water until it reaches half way up the cake pan.
> Bake in the middle of the oven for 45 - 60 minutes or until the top is golden and the custard is set. Let it cool slightly. Serve warm.

Serves 4.

Gardening is not only a tonic to the soul and soothing to the mind, but is an excellent workout as well, burning up to 500 calories an hour.

# Strawberries Supreme

The sauce in this recipe is also good over a slice of Angel Food cake. Lemon juice and lemon rind may be substituted for the orange juice and rind.

2 cup strawberries, washed, hulled, cut in half
1 Tablespoon sugar
1/2 cup sugar
2 teaspoons grated orange rind
1/2 cup orange juice
1 cup heavy cream, whipped

A sherbet and a sorbet are basically the same thing, but most sherbets have a little milk or egg white added to the fruit purée. Ices are fruit juice, sweetener and water frozen in an ice cream machine. They are generally more watery than a sorbet. Frapeé is a fruit sherbet frozen hard and pressed through a strainer when it is slightly thawed to give it a slushy texture. Ice cream is smooth because it contains a high perecntage of butter fat. Vanilla ice cream must have at least 10% butterfat and chocolate must have 8% butterfat to qualify as an ice cream by the FDA. If it has less than that it is called ice milk.

A wine sorbet can be used between courses as a palate cleanser.

When choosing a sweetener remember that sugar has less taste than honey. The new gourmet honeys often have very strong flavors.

-Susan

> Put strawberries in a small bowl and sprinkle with 1 Tablespoon sugar.
> In a small saucepan, combine the 1/2 cup sugar, orange juice and orange rind and bring to a boil. Stir until the sugar dissolves, then gently simmer without stirring for 10 minutes. Let cool completely.
> At serving time, whip the cream and fold it into the orange syrup.
> Put the berries into individual serving bowls and top with a generous spoonful of orange cream.

Serves 4.

## Fresh Fruit Sorbet

I have made this sorbet with a large variety of fruits and it has always been delicious. Pick whatever is plentiful and ripe.

*1 - 2 quarts of fresh fruit*
*sugar or honey*
*2 Tablespoons lemon juice*
*fruit liqueur*

> Freeze fruit. Do not freeze solid. If your fruit is frozen solid, allow it to thaw a bit before processing.
> In a food processor fitted with a metal blade, purée the fruit in small batches at a time. Between each batch empty purée into a bowl.
> After all of the fruit is processed, taste and sweeten to your palate.
> Add 2 Tablespoons lemon juice and any fruit liqueur you like as an additional flavor enhancer, but do not over do.

>Freeze again. 30 minutes before serving remove from freezer to soften. Just prior to serving purée again.

# Ice Cream Torte

1 package Angel Flake coconut, sweetened
1 cup almonds, blanched and finely chopped
2 eggs whites
1 quart chocolate ice cream, softened
1 quart coffee ice cream, softened
fudge sauce
1 crushed toffee candy bar

>Preheat oven to 350°.
>Butter bottom of a 10 inch springform pan.
>Beat egg whites until soft peaks form.
>Fold coconut and almonds into egg whites. Line bottom of pan with the mixture.
>Bake until lightly browned. Let cool.
>Empty the quart of softened chocolate ice cream on top of crust, spreading smoothly. Freeze briefly.
>Coat with fudge sauce. Add the quart of coffee ice cream to the layers and top with the remainder of the fudge sauce.
>Sprinkle with chopped toffee candy and freeze at least 4 hours or until firm.

## Fudge Sauce

1/2 stick butter
3/4 cocoa powder, unsweetened, Droste or Hershey
1/2 cup golden brown sugar

**Favorite Liqueurs**
**Curacao** is an inexpensive orange flavored liqueur.
**Cointreau** and **Triple Sec** are also orange flavored but a bit more expensive.
**Fraise** is a French liqueur from strawberries.
**Framboise** is also from France but made from raspberries. It is a very strong flavored liqueur.
**Calvados** is a French apple brandy.
**Applejack** is the American version which is not as rich bodied.
**Tia Maria** and **Kahlua** are coffee flavored liqueurs.
**Cassis** is made from currants.
**Creme de Cocoa** is chocolate flavored, while
**Creme de Menthe** has a very minty taste.
**Sambuca** has a wonderful anise flavor and is usually served with three coffee beans in the bottom of the glass for luck.

**Ignorance doesn't kill you, but it makes you sweat a lot.**
. . . Haitian Proverb

Creme fraiche is a heavy cultured cream. It has been thickened and allowed to develop a delicate sour taste, giving it a tart edge. It has a variety of uses; it can be dolloped over dessert and berries, added to sauces for richness, or spooned over vegetables as a simple sauce. Because it can be cooked without fear of separation, it has greater versatility than sour cream. It also can be stored in the refrigerator for up to two weeks.

*1/2 cup half and half*
*2 Tablespoons corn syrup*
*1 teaspoon vanilla*

> Heat all ingredients, except vanilla, together over medium high heat until sauce reaches rolling boil.
> Remove from heat and add vanilla.
> Allow to cool slightly before layering on ice cream torte, according to directions above.

## Creme Fraiche

*1 cup heavy cream (not ultra pasteurized)*
*1 cup dairy sour cream*

> Whisk the two creams together in a bowl.
> Cover the bowl and let stand in a warm place overnight.
> Place in a covered container and refrigerate for at least 8 hours. The longer the mixture remains in the refrigerator, the tarter the flavor. The creme fraiche should be quite thick.

# Turtleback Facts

Turtleback Farm is a country inn located on Orcas Island, considered by most to be the loveliest of the islands that dot the San Juan archipelago in the sparkling waters of Puget Sound. The inn overlooks eighty acres of forest and farmland in the shadow of Turtleback Mountain (discernible from the ferry that brings passengers from Friday Harbor). It commands a spectacular view of lush meadows, duck ponds and outbuildings with Mt. Constitution providing the backdrop to the east.

The inn is centrally located in beautiful Crow Valley, 6 miles from the ferry landing and close to Moran State Park. There are many recreational activities on the island; golfing, wind surfing, sea kayaking, moped and bicycle rentals, fresh water fishing and swimming in the park, charter boats for saltwater fishing, cruising and sailing, fascinating artisans and shops, and many excellent restaurants. Bill and Susan Fletcher, the proprietors, will be happy to help in the planning of your activities.

Orcas Island is accessible by ferries from Anacortes and Victoria, B.C. or by Lake Union Airlines. There is no public transportation on the island.

Reservations should be made well ahead for the inn is often booked weeks in advance. Room rates are based on double occupancy and all rooms have a private bath. Rates may vary seasonally. Breakfast for two is included in the price of the room. Because of the rural nature of Turtleback Farm, the inn cannot accept pets. Children are accepted by special arrangement only.

For further information about the inn or to make reservations please call or write:

Turtleback Farm Inn
Route 1 Box 650
Eastsound, WA 98245
(206) 376-4914

# Index

# Travel Notes

# Travel Notes

If you would like to have your own copy of this wonderful cookbook or perhaps purchase a few as gifts, we have included the simple order form below.

\_\_\_\_\_ $10.95     Turtleback Farm Inn Cookbook

The adventures of the Traveling Gourmets continue with the 2nd and 3rd in the series, cookbooks with the fabulous recipes of the *Carter House and Hotel Carter* in Eureka, California, and *The Herbfarm* in Snoqualmie Valley, Washington.

\_\_\_\_\_ $10.95     Carter House / Hotel Carter Cookbook
                      (release date is May, 1991)

\_\_\_\_\_ $10.95     The Herbfarm Cookbook
                      (release date is July 1991)

\_\_\_\_\_ \_\_\_\_\_     Total for Books
\_\_\_\_\_ \_\_\_\_\_     Postage & Shipping ( $1 per book )
\_\_\_\_\_ \_\_\_\_\_     TOTAL

- - - - - - - - - - - - - - - - - - - - - - - - - - - - - - - - -

Please Print:

Name _____

Address _____

_____

City_____ State \_\_\_ Zip Code \_\_\_\_\_

Mail Your Check or Money Order To:

Sweet Forever Publishing
P.O. Box 1000
10 Myth Road
Eastsound, WA 98245
(206) 376-2809